Southwestern Women: New Voices

Southwestern Women

New Voices

Javelina Press ⁊ Tucson, Arizona

Grateful acknowledgment is given to the following:
Excerpt from *Women Who Run With the Wolves* by Clarissa Pinkola Estés, Ph.D.,
Copyright © 1992, 1995. Reprinted by kind permission of Dr. Estés, and Ballantine
Books, a division of Random House, Inc.
Excerpt from "The Narrow Roads of Oku" is from the collection *Dwarf Bamboo* by
Marilyn Chin, Copyright © 1987. Reprinted by kind permission of The Greenfield
Review Press.

Address inquiries to:
Javelina Press
P.O. Box 42131
Tucson, AZ 85733

04 03 02 01 00 99 98   5 4 3 2

ISBN 0-9654418-3-0

Library of Congress Catalog Card Number 96-78474

Cataloging-in-Publication Data:
Southwestern Women: New Voices / edited by Caitlin L. Gannon.
    Includes bibliography.
    1. Women--Southwestern United States--Literary collections. 2. Southwestern
United States--Literature. 3. American literature--Women authors.

Cover illustration: "La Frontera" © 1997 by Virginia L. Westray.
Cover designed by Nancy Serensky.

Printed in the United States of America on acid-free recycled paper.

to all the people who supported and encouraged me with this book,
my deepest gratitude

especially
Virginia Westray, best friend and mother,
whose example taught me to trust my creative voice
William Gannon, for always believing this project was important and possible
and Jim, for being my favorite brother

Contents

Introduction

This anthology spotlights the work of contemporary women writers whose lives have been significantly shaped by their experiences of the Southwest. In recent years, Southwestern writing has grown in popularity and many authors have received widespread recognition and exposure. This collection emphasizes newer writings, by women, that have not yet been widely published or anthologized.

I am proud to introduce the work of 30 women writers of the Southwest, published here for the first time. Some of the contributors already have long-established writing careers, and for others this is a debut publication. Eloquently, painfully, and humorously, their words explore the connections between place and identity, and their powerful imagery gives us new insight into the complexities of Southwestern culture. At the same time, these writings celebrate the differences between women on a more universal scale.

Before discussing the work presented in this volume, I would like to briefly place this anthology in its historical context, in order to highlight the importance of recognizing new work as well as new writers. From the diaries and letters of early frontier women in the 1800's to new developments in contemporary Southwestern poetry and fiction, women writers have had a strong voice in shaping the character of Southwestern literature. Historically, the Southwest has often been portrayed in literature from an outsider's perspective, which either mythologized the Wild West, or romanticized the simple, uncorrupted nature of the region's indigenous cultures. Early portrayals of the Southwest in literature, by women and men, reflected the cultural tensions and stereotypes that marked relations between Anglos, Spanish Americans, Mexicans and Native Americans since the first interactions between these groups. In recent decades, however, writers from the Southwest have worked to inscribe their own realities into this literature. Women writers stand at the forefront of the movement to develop Southwestern literature into a culturally diverse and distinctive body of writing.

The region first gained national recognition as an important arts center in the 1920's, when prominent writers and artists began to flock to the Southwest, primarily New Mexico, to escape the chaotic urban existence of the East and reconnect with more "natural" ways of living. These artists, including such writers as D.H. Lawrence and Witter Bynner, were drawn to the Southwest by the allure of its Native American and Hispanic cultures, and by the stunningly different beauty of the landscape.

Women writers were quite prominent in this period of literary growth, as this new environment allowed them to dedicate themselves to the promotion of new forms of poetry and literary expression. Alice Corbin Henderson, Mary Austin, Mabel Dodge Luhan, and Willa Cather were among the most well-known Santa Fe writers in the 20's. Their writings reflect their admiration of the land and their appreciation for the oral traditions and poetry of the Southwest's native cultures. The enduring popularity of their works has ensured a strong feminine presence in the literary canon of the West.

Women's literature of the Southwest, like the arts of the 1920's in general, was largely an Anglo-dominated field. In the 30's and 40's, however, a group of Hispanic writers emerged on the scene and began to explore their connections to the Southwest through writing. The three most well-known Hispanic female authors of the mid-century are Fabiola Cabeza de Baca, Nina Otero-Warren and Cleofas Jaramillo. They wrote in Spanish and in English, attempting through language to heal the split between the two cultures of their worlds. They connected the American Southwest with its history as a part of Mexico, a point of departure which contrasted sharply with earlier Anglo writers' portrayals of the region as an undeveloped frontier.

With the emergence of both the civil and women's rights movements, Southwestern literature continued to develop a multifaceted character. Writers began to focus on the difficult task of integrating and celebrating different cultures, histories and languages through writing, using women's voices as well as men's. New authors that emerged on the literary scene included more Native American and Hispanic/Chicana writers, who had previously been spoken for and about but had not had the opportunity to nurture their own means of creative expression in literature.

Today, Southwestern women writers such as Paula Gunn Allen, Gloria Anzaldúa, Ana Castillo, Denise Chavez, Sandra Cisneros, Joy Harjo, Barbara Kingsolver, Demetria Martinez, and Leslie Marmon Silko are internationally known for their work, in which they give voice to the many histories and faces of the Southwest. The bibliography at the end of this collection will guide you to the work of many more of the women who have been so important in shaping the diverse and vibrant character of Southwestern literature over the centuries.

In organizing this anthology, my intent was to categorize the pieces thematically into chapters, according to aspects of life such as spirituality, family, or culture. I discovered, however, that the writing was all interwoven in some way with each of these themes, and resisted such classification. I therefore let the pieces determine their own arrangement.

The collection begins with Maria Teresa Garcia's sensual and mystical poem "Recamara Mexicana," followed by Margo Tamez' conjuration of the voices of attentive spirits. Susan Chamberlin Quick captures the complexity of the desert in her poem "Sorting Burdens." In "Riding Home," Laura Tohe shares with the reader memories of life on the Navajo Reservation through a journey back home to visit her father. In Susan San Miguel's "Papá Sits Outside," female characters are constrained by the contradictory position of women in a traditional Hispanic family, in which femininity is both exalted and suppressed. Antonia Quintana Pigno presents a powerful illumination of the difficult bond between parent and child, and the depth of loss and longing brought on by death.

The female body of the desert and its beauty becomes the subject of Lyndsey Cronk's visual and textual imagery in "Fertile Ground." Emilie Vardaman writes of building a new life on the Mexican border, and watching how it transforms from an arbitrary but gentle division between countries into a painful steel wall. In "A Chant for Remembrance," Elizabeth Ann Galligan celebrates the memory of renowned anthropologist Bertha Pauline Dutton and her return to the land she held so sacred. Sherry Luna, writing at the death bed of a grandfather, explores different spiritual approaches to questions as difficult as death. Laura Tohe's poem "Salt River" speaks to the creative powers of Earth, and in "Grand Canyon," Judith McDaniel experiences Nature's awesome test, psychological and physical, of human endurance.

Rita Garitano's narrator, through the ritual of washing her mother's hair, reflects on this woman's emotional distance and her inability to understand her daughter's world. In Maria Leyba's "The Last Supper," a child struggles to understand the execution of a prisoner at the state penitentiary where she and her family live in employee housing. J.M. Kore Salvato's "Salvage Yard" juxtaposes a teenage runaway, a Vietnam vet and illegal aliens working in a junkyard in a compelling exploration of hope, loss, and survival. Maria Leyba's poem "Emergence" reflects on a powerful journey from a life shrouded in violence toward reclaiming a family's self-reliance and pride. Carla Jean Eardley evokes a strong image of an independent woman trying to maintain control of her rough-edged world. Glenda Stewart Langley's "Cooking Beans" is a deeply moving portrait of love and the appreciation of simplicity.

Jacqueline Moody offers an eloquent and image-rich treatment of the loss of a loved one to cancer in "Moving Towards Morning." Next, Jessica Jaramillo's "Los Tucsonenses" gives us a glimpse into the many facets of life in Tucson's Mexican-American community. In Sharon Creeden's poem "Patchwork Life," a simple quilt artfully reflects images of the poet's life and personality.

In "Russian Wedding," Maria-Elena Wakamatsu reflects on what it means to have a homeland as she recalls her childhood in Yuma, Arizona, while visiting the Soviet Union. Evamaria Lugo's narrator in "Light at Dusk" struggles to accept rather than doubt the completeness of her lover's devotion. Carmela Delia Lanza's lyrical poem "Grace" evokes cycles of life, death and renewal, while Sharon DiMaria conjures characters rich with life through memories of old relatives and family celebrations past. Jill Oglesby writes of growing up Anglo in Albuquerque, and her search for the physical evidence that would connect her birth to the land that is her home. From the spectacle of molting coyotes to shopping for bargains across the border, Lorraine Ray gives a humorous look at characters and artifacts common in the Southwest.

In Alicia Z. Galván's "Vegetables," the narrator remembers lessons she learned through a childhood in poverty, such as the appreciation of abundance in whatever imperfect form it takes. In her search for a path to her cultural roots, Dolissa Medina vividly invokes the mythical image of La Sirena, "an oceanic curandera" who inhabits two worlds, land and sea, bridging the gap between the two. Theresa Delgadillo writes in "Go Ahead" of the defiant spirit of a Los Angeles garment worker on trial for the murder of her employer. Next, set against a backdrop of crystal healings and leftist activism in "Granola Whites, Polyester Indians," Gloria Dyc explores the human struggle to overcome the forces that are out of control in our environment, be they breast cancer, tribal land rights, or a marriage.

Finally, Lorenza de Zavala-Wheeler writes of a childhood marked by "cross-cultural distress," and the powerful reconnection with her cultural heritage that results from visiting the Southwest and later living near the Mexican border as an adult. The land is deeply connected, physically and spiritually, to the history of the people who have lived here. It is from the energy and tension of this interconnection that individual and cultural identity emerges. "The first causes of my being lie in the antiquity of Mexico," Zavala-Wheeler writes, "And yet I have only come this far, just to the edge, where I look over the line with sadness and dismay, as though into a void."

The marks on the land, like the ugliness of the border, are the marks of our own histories, painfully present and inescapable. Yet the land, as Zavala-Wheeler says, is also an abundant source of healing and strength: "What more satisfying existence could I construct than what I've made here so far, a coincidence of solitude and peace, a garden inside the cracked walls, my books and music, the infinitely changing light on the mountains?"

Are you back in your bed
as I am in mine?
In this pura Mexicana bedroom
where I burn white candles
for purity and copal to soothe
the spirits,
where Frida and the Madonna
sit on the nightstand to my left,
where the Girl from Puebla
dressed in her China Poblana
(like the one I wore as a child)
hangs over the heavy black iron bed.
Where a dancing tin skeleton
smiles from between white eyelet curtains
reminding me of my own mortality,
where in the window
is a double shadow box,
on one side, the Sacred Heart
encircled with a crown of thorns,
on the other, La Virgen de Guadalupe
in the colors of the Mexican flag.

We have a saying:
Santo que no es visto no es adorado,
A saint who is not seen is not worshipped.

Some people might hesitate to make
love beneath so many eyes.
It has never bothered me.

The Sacred Papers of Guerrero Pueblo

Margo Jamez

1.

Fig juices stain your fingers
and I could lick them like I'd suck deeply
on any holy man's wound.

—Sing me your prayer

—Hombre de Tonatiuh, Espiritu Santo...

Your chicken blood sings in the right key
I promise to watch
as papeles de Guerrero curl and twist

—Smoke of sage lift my prayers
to the ceiling of the spirits' desires...

2.

Indio de Guerrero pueblo...
arousing us Spirits to dance with shadows
encoded in messages rising from ash of
smoke to man and woman.

Tonatiuh smiles for your remembrance
that holy days are real for spirits
when the journey back promises cigaros y mescal
y candelarios, yes!

Lure us dead to our images on brown paper
seduce us into the flicker that promises fire
to the realm of some-more
another taste of flesh for just a flash
to that feeling that waits that opens that engulfs
try to catch us, we'll play! we'll play!

Ayy! But hold on holy man!
Don't take your loving labor so serious *trovero.*
Spirit warrior, it's your feet which bear the weight of clay
and ours are free to float,
coming and going, we have many vistas to visit
so many Guerreros pounding,
bark of fig howling for our replies,
making sounds only dancing shadows know
are prayers to you
but intoxication to us.
We have many cigaros and mescal gulps to take
don't trap us...!

Only holy days we can travel farther.
Dancing under a moon that caresses
the land that feeds the spirit
who blesses your prayers which cry
for answers that live on the other side of shadows.

Sorting Burdens

Susan Chamberlin Quick

We bring these old stones,
life clinging to
life carrying burdens
from each's recent past
under the Desert's skin to bury.

Adding to Her horny needlepoint face
hearts small and hard as curled souls
rising from this task to deliver,
again and again.

Earning the night's smile we stand
spread arms to the sky,
fingertips draw feathers from the air.

Distilled in Her future and
Desert dreams of lofty
flight, clear water, ample grain.

We are sorting burdens, my sisters,
by whose measure?

Riding Home
Laura Tohe

I SHIFT into park and turn off the engine. Most of the time he's inside when I visit. I knock at the wooden door facing east that has started to peel in layers the way mud curls after it dries. "Dad, it's me." After a short pause, he opens the door and passes through it bending a little as he does, the way the Anasazi must've passed through their doorways. He takes my hand and then embraces me heartily. "Yá'át'ééh shitsi'. Nílái yee naaltsoos yíshta nt'ę́ę́'. (I was just reading the newspaper.)" He seems a little embarrassed to be visited upon in the middle of the day caught in the act of reading. Better to be caught in the act of working, chopping wood, painting chairs, mending fences. Something that shows visibility of labor. We sit on one of the rickety wooden benches near the silver watertanks outside his hogan. He takes his place nearest the petrified logs. He has neither running water, electricity nor television; he lives a simple life. A small butane tank connected by a metal hose leads into the hogan where a yellow gas stove cooks his meals. That and the little newspaper box with "The Independent" written on it near the highway are the only visible signs of his connection to the outside world even though he lives only a short distance from the highway.

At age four he bought me ice cream cones. I turn the cone upside down and watch the mushy sweet white stuff splat onto the ground leaving an oozy mess. I only liked to eat the cone. My mother's voice: "Éí dí doo éí yíyáada. (That one doesn't eat ice cream.) She always does that." The memory of him buying me a luxury food stays with me because we could rarely afford it. Another time he arrived home with a bag full of groceries and a wooden crate of peaches sitting in green tissue cups like little gifts. He presents them as a peace offering to my mother who had long since ceased to be impressed by him.

He tells me stories. The day the steel electricity carriers were installed east of his hogan. His voice is animated by how he saw the helicopters hover above the ground like dragon flies, and helped place the steel girders into the earth that resemble the shapes of Navajo sacred beings, Yei. The electricity gods carry power from the Four Corners to feed the cities in the Southwest through the steel webs strung past his land. He never mentions the irony. It was the story that is most important, as if he too were drawing power from the current flowing through the steel umbilical cord.

I'm lying in his bed. The fire crackles in the potbelly stove. The kerosene lamp casts a dim glow in the hogan. Nulí (paternal grandmother) spreads Menthol-atum on her chest and the smell pervades the room. It's the smell of grandmothers weathering cold stiff winters. "Nítsi' daatsí yídlóh? (Maybe your daughter's cold?)" she says, rubbing more Mentholatum on her neck. He leans over me and pulls the corduroy and denim quilt up to cover my shoulders. That's when I learn what it means to be tucked in. "I'm okay, Daddy." He smiles toward me. Nulí and Daddy chat awhile longer. After a pause, he turns on the flashlight. That's his way of saying good night, because Navajos have no word for good night. He turns down the lamp until it grows dim. The room darkens except for the circle of light cast from the flashlight. He closes the door behind him to find his bed in Nulí's other house.

Today I'm curious about his childhood before he joined the Marines during World War II at the illegal age of 16. The dog trots by as if wanting to be noticed; a little gray mutt, the kind found on any reservation. Sometimes if trained right, they make good sheep dogs, chasing after the stray ones or the ones that lag behind. "That one's name is Kalabee," he says as if he was naming a variety of tomato in his garden. Once known as Character when he was a city dog and my brother had him, he renamed him with a Navajo pronunciation. Kalabee gives us a sideways glance when he hears his name, then disappears behind the house. Navajos believe dogs belong outside and not curled up on the bed or next to the fire the way white people allow their animals inside.

Though dogs lead harsh lives, they are also well regarded for being good sentinels, barking at the first sound of an approaching car or an unrecognized visitor. Sometimes my father boiled a skillet full of leftovers into a gravy mixture and poured it into the dog dish. He believes in the loyalty of dogs.

"I went to Saint Catherine's in Santa Fe. Those nuns were tough. They used to make us walk down the aisle on our knees. Then we had to pray." He swats a fly that lands on the watertank. He shakes it loose from the plastic mesh. "It was hard on the knees. After a couple of months I got sick of that place." He's always been somewhat of a rebel. He laughs. "I told this boy I was gonna run away. He said 'I'll go with you.' He's from around Crownpoint." He sticks his chin out toward that direction because it's rude for Navajos to point with their finger. "I got home and stayed around, then I went to Ganado." He still runs from the missionaries that come periodically carrying the Bible or Book of Mormon, or he just doesn't answer the door. Sometimes just to be ornery, he shouts from behind the closed door, "go away, we're all heathens!" Our relatives that live just up the road avoid the missionaries as if they were tax auditors. They run to the outhouse knowing they won't be followed. Ironically, arthritis settles into his knees as if God was playing a joke on him for running away.

By the light of the kerosene lamp he taught my cousin and me how to play blackjack one summer. "Hit me, ji'nii," he instructs us when we want another card. Nulí tries to sleep and grows impatient with us. "Noo'jee" (go to bed) she scolds from under her quilts, but we are having too much fun. He knocks on the oil cloth covered table. "I'm good." Tonight we are all children.

Sometimes he drank too much. Leaving to chase the bottles in Gallup, Flagstaff, Albuquerque, Farmington. Getting booze on Sunday was only a matter of a trip to the Arizona stateline. It was called going to The Stateline because New Mexico didn't sell alcohol on Sundays. That broken down building near the highway was all too eager to sell to Indians, underage or not.

In the summer evenings as we drove the cattle, he sang us home with riding songs. My father's song pushing the end of the day to a close. His voice merging with the sagebrush, the rocks, the horses, and into our hearts.

The hogan listens to the sounds of the highway. The hogan remembers the sound of newspapers rustling, meat sizzling in the skillet, enamel dishes being put away, dogs barking, the sound of chopping wood. A fire burning.

Papá Sits Outside

Susan San Miguel

PAPÁ LOOKS a little bit lonely sitting out there on the front porch. That's his favorite chair. It's a barber shop chair, blue vinyl but it looks like a la-z-boy. He's had it propped up on the front porch for as long as I can remember and he just sits in it watching the world go by or reading about it in the newspaper. Sometimes when my oldest brother Marco passes by Papá'll ask him questions like what about that new tax law or who do you think will win the next city council election. He never asks me anything because he thinks I'm too young to read the paper and besides I'm a girl.

Papá hardly ever comes in the house anymore except to sleep or maybe he just stays out there all night. It used to be my uncles would come over and they'd all stand around or lean against Papá's old Chevy pickup as if they were all Mr. Suave and they'd drink beers and smoke these thin little cigarettes that made them look like they should be in some old Hollywood movie, and they'd eye the pretty girls walking past.

Then there would come Maria Garcia or Esperanza Ramón wearing their slinky black miniskirts with lots of ruffles around their hips and shoulders and their skinny high heels and their hair poofed out like more ruffles and their big raccoon eyes peeping out of black eyeliner. My uncles would stop talking, then they'd put their hands in their pockets and give those girls the once over, up and down from toe to head and back. They'd be pretty drunk by that time so they'd start taunting my little brother who is only six years old, asking him to take a drink of their beer because it'd make him stronger, then he could kiss Maria and be a man. Maria would glance over her shoulder like she was about to swat a fly but then she would catch Uncle Jo's eye and smile and wink.

"Aaay, she wants you little one," and Uncle Jo would push Juanito out in the street towards her.

Poor Juanito, he would just stare sheepishly at his toes and wait for Mamá who was always nearby to save him. As soon as he saw her he would run for her skirts. She would hear them laughing and run outside and chase my uncles away with a broom. You should have seen her sweeping them off the porch like little roly-poly bugs. And they were afraid of her too; their eyes said so. After my sister Cecilia's wedding, when they all got so drunk they couldn't even stand she told them they could never come back here again and they haven't so Papá just sits, all by himself.

Papá is known to be a very wise man. The angels that watch over our house swoop down from their perches in the trees and on the telephone wires and whisper secrets to him while he sleeps and that's why he knows so much. He can tell you things, like when the next storm will come or if you will have good luck or if your son should marry a particular girl. If you let my Papá touch your new baby no harm will come to it. All the people who have bad times, Mamá used to say if Papá could just touch these people they'd be all right. It's for this reason that all of us are so healthy. She says if it wasn't for Papá, Juanito might not have even lived. Mamá was sicker than ever before with Juanito so the whole family traveled to the church of San Juan in the valley. During the trip Papá would pat Mamá's belly and say that God was with her and when they got there we all prayed that Mamá's baby would live. Now every year on Juanito's saint's day we go there and say a prayer. Mamá says it was Papá's prayers that counted the most.

"Papá, what're you doing?" I asked him. He had been sitting there so long with his hands on his knees. We were the only ones home. Cecilia took Mamá to her house to look at dress patterns.

"Whaaa?" He couldn't hear very well and he wouldn't buy a hearing aid even though the insurance would pay for it. "Sure is a pretty day isn't it little one?" and he patted my hand.

"Yea, sure is a pretty day." He used to talk only in spurts, but now he hardly talks at all, not since Cecilia got married. I didn't know what to say to him. We sat there in silence for maybe five minutes until he spoke again, startling me so much that my shoulders shook and my scalp tingled.

"A man is going to take you away some day, I guess," he sighed. "Don't let him get to you."

I thought he would continue but there was only silence. "What did you say Papá?" Then he looked at me angrily and shook his head. I wanted to go to him and tell him I wouldn't let a man ever get me, but he raised his hand toward me so abruptly as if to slap me away.

"Get away from me," he growled.
Frightened, I ran into the kitchen searching for my mother just as she and Cecilia entered through the back door.

"Mamá, tonight I'm going to cook dinner with a Hawaiian theme, like this here," Cecilia was saying, and she pointed to a woman's magazine that had a picture of this white lady wearing one of those fancy little shirtwaist dresses like Lucy would wear for Ricky in reruns of the *I Love Lucy Show*. The lady had on a Hawaiian apron with bananas and pineapples printed daintily on its borders and a big smile as she raised a tray of more pineapples to her audience. "Create Ambiance: Have a Little Vacation for Dinner," read the caption. I watched my big sister with interest.

"And I think I'll wear this colorful dress that I bought at the flea market last year. Do you think it's close enough? See, the colors are the same."

Mamá glanced at the dress and the picture and said that she thought that was a wonderful idea but was *he* going to eat only pineapples and bananas for dinner.

"What about the meat or the tortillas?" she asked.

"Silly Mamá, here's the recipe on the next page for pineapple glazed chicken. That's what I'll cook."

"But pineapples aren't in season right now." Mamá looked at her, perplexed. How would Cecilia manage this one?

"Mamá, I'll buy canned pineapples. See here, the recipe calls for two cans of pineapples."

"Oh yes," Mamá answered slowly as she glanced at the recipe, impressed. "I had forgotten." Cecilia looked so excited.

"Well, I better get started," and she left, happy.

~ ~ ~

When Cecilia turned eighteen she got a job at the little grocery store only two blocks away. With the money she bought a car even though Papá had said no and then she started wearing pretty dresses with embroidery on them and sandals with beads; her hair she wore down, thick and dark, no more braids. Almost every night she went downtown all by herself and listened to the Mariachis and read her poetry about women who slid down to the earth on moonbeams to find love. She read to the men who passed through from Mexico, and when she came home she talked to them on the phone. She read an entire romance to Hector, a man who came to work in the states to send money back home. I would sit at the kitchen table pretending to do my homework but really I listened to my big sister read to Hector.

Perched on the kitchen stool, all dressed up as if she were on a date and he could see her, her flowing red dress spread over her legs and the stool like a Christmas bell, she read, "She searched in his dark and ravaged face for the slightest spark of emotion but there was none. But he did love her. He must love her, she knew he loved her," her voice intense with drama. "Oh Hector, Querido," I heard her whisper into the telephone, pausing, playing with the wisp of thick black hair that fell close to her cheek, "Do you think he really did love her?"

"Si, si," his voice loud and excited spilled eagerly from the phone into our kitchen, into Cecilia's lap.

Cecilia smiled and continued, "She would make him love her."

I wondered what Hector thought, if he could even understand Cecilia. As far as I knew he spoke only Spanish, but Cecilia and the rest of her friends from high school insisted on English. She was improving herself, she announced regularly. She was going to get a job as a secretary in a big office building downtown and she would be able to buy all of her own things. She wouldn't have to depend on Papá anymore; she would be independent. I looked up from where I pretended to be studying and saw Papá's arm stretched like a barrier across the doorway. Trapped in the kitchen with Cecilia, I didn't want to see the rest of him. He too had been listening to Cecilia on the telephone. He knew of her plans to leave.

"Listen to our daughter," he yelled into the living room as he stared steadily at Cecilia. "Do you hear what kind of woman she is becoming?" Before Mamá could stop him, Papá marched angrily up to her and tore the open book from Cecilia's hand.

"Ouch! You pulled my hair," she screamed. Cecilia's hair, flowing like dark river waves, was the thing she was the most proud of. But then she backed off. Papá's face, it had changed from the playful sometimes stern face I was used to seeing to something hard and unreal, a chunk of red brick chipped from our very own house. Papá moved closer, an inch away from her face, staring at her with steel eyes, daring her not to be afraid of him. He raised his hand as if to slap her. Cecilia didn't move; she didn't even seem to be breathing. She looked him straight in the eye. His voice thunderous and hollow saying all those things about Cecilia in Spanish. "Puta," he called her. Cecilia, so shocked she forgot, couldn't move to hang up the phone. Hector heard. Hector heard. Oh Angels in heaven, en el cielo, en la tierra and in our yard, please do not let this happen to me.

Hector stayed away for a few days, but then he returned. She said their love was forever, and that they would soon be married. He bought her a wedding dress, antique white. The very next week he fled to his wife in Mexico.

Papá moved from the couch to the porch.

Why would Hector spend all that money on a dress and then just leave I wondered. She bewitched him; she put a spell on him to get what she wanted, I heard Papá's thought but no one else did.

He and Mamá fought all the time then, while Juanito and I hid under the covers. I tried to protect my little brother by playing games. The fan on the ceiling whirls round and round and the cu cuy races through its shadows. It doesn't know that it's only going round and round, in and out between the blades. When it figures this out it will fly from its circle and get you. His eyes fixed on the motion of the fan.

"I see the cu cuy and it won't get out," he giggled and watched and watched until he fell asleep, never noticing the anger in the next room. They yelled at the top of their voices as if another language would prevent others from hearing them. Papá said that Mamá didn't respect him anymore, that she no longer did what he told her to do. They were arguing about Cecilia. Mamá said that she knew what was best for her daughter, she had given her life after all. He wouldn't listen.

He left. While he was gone I felt the quiet, all alone. What if Papá never returned? What would it be like if Mamá and Papá weren't married? Things would not be the same. Cecilia and I would live with Mamá and Marco and Juanito with Papá and maybe we would never see each other again. Then I wouldn't have to worry about what Papá thought of me and they wouldn't yell so much or make fun of Juanito but Mamá wouldn't cook for all of us and Papá wouldn't always get the biggest piece of meat because he wouldn't be here but that meant Mamá would have to go to work and I would have to do all the work at home because

Cecilia never does anything. I sure would miss us all. I sat on the front porch and waited for him. Three days later he returned, silent. Mamá hid her eyes and did what he wanted.

A day or two later Cecilia went out again, at night. Mamá raised her eyes and said she's a young girl and needs to have fun and what's the harm in that. Besides, she hasn't been out for so long. Papá grimaced and shook his head but he didn't say anything. That night Cecilia didn't come home at all. She called at three in the morning and spoke to Papá. She had been kidnapped by a dangerous man who had raped her. She hung up the phone. Gone. Papá said she must have had to sneak that phone call and then was discovered. That's why she hung up so quickly. Tears filled his eyes.

"Dios mio! My child!" Papá exclaimed. "I'll kill him." He looked up at us, ready for action. Something was expected of him and he knew what he had to do. He left and returned with all of his brothers and they sat in silence and waited for the phone to ring again. They had guns. So many of them, like an army. They sat on every piece of furniture, guns steady on their knees. Every once and awhile they would glance at each other and nod importantly. A man had forced himself on an innocent woman, one of their own, family.

Mamá, quiet and respectful, asked if anybody wanted coffee. Everybody said no.

Juanito and I got to stay up all night on this important occasion to find out our sister's fate. I couldn't help myself; I was very excited.

Uncle Jo interrupted the silence with a little uncomfortable laugh. "Women," he said. "Who knows what they'll do next? eh?" Nobody answered. Nobody thought it was funny.

"My little girl," Papá cried. "Someone has... has..." He couldn't finish the sentence.

The phone rang again. It was Cecilia. She was happy. She said he was going to marry her and they would arrive soon to meet the family and have breakfast.

The uncles got up from their chairs then some of them sat down again, then got up again and sat down and walked around, always looking down at the floor or at each other, not at Papá. They were afraid to look at Papá. Finally they put their guns in the back bedroom and tried to talk about other things, the baseball game next week against Saint Lawrence's parish.

Poor Papá. He seemed to wither away like an old dead weed just at the sound of Cecilia's voice on the phone. He sighed and went outside maybe so none of us would look at him and see his sadness.

Mamá cooked breakfast. She cooked huevos rancheros, and cut a fresh melon from the garden. She made tortillas and pico de gallo and sent me to the store for orange juice and more milk so that we would certainly have enough. We all went to the bedroom window to look out when we heard the crunching of their feet on the gravelly driveway and then shy whispering.

"Papá, this is Antonio," Cecilia said. Her voice shook a little.

Papá didn't say anything, just looked him straight in the eye and nodded.

"Mucho gusto, Señor," Antonio stuck out his hand for a handshake.

Papá took it grudgingly, barely touching. Then he got up from his chair and went inside, too quickly. Mamá had to run in from the bedroom. Then we all came in, little by little, Cecilia introducing each one of us as we entered. Antonio nodded again and again and said mucho gusto. I know he couldn't remember all of our names. He held Cecilia's hand stiffly, self-consciously. He never let go of it the whole time. He held it under the table even while he ate. I watched Papá watch their hands.

Mamá made a motion for Antonio to sit down. He sat down. He ate slowly, seeming to savor each bit, all of us staring at him expectantly.

"Muy sabrosa," he said to Mamá.
We all shifted and nodded and continued to look at him.

A hot breeze blew through the kitchen windows and past our heads. It lifted the strands of hair that fell near Cecilia's cheeks, then fluttered the paper napkins on the table until Mamá quieted them with the arrangement of silk roses that Cecilia had made at her flower arranging class last summer.

Papá asked hesitantly, "When will the wedding take place?"
"Next week," Cecilia answered.

Then very deliberately he asked, "And how will you be married in the church? Father Hernandez will not tolerate such short notice. He must prepare you for the sacrament of marriage so that you are ready in the eyes of God."

"Papá, we must get married next week. We must," Cecilia pleaded desperately but her husband-to-be did not look up from his eggs and tortillas.

"I will speak with the Padre," Mamá said.
"It's just not right," Papá answered, glaring at Mamá and he walked out on the porch and sat down. Mamá followed. We all listened but their sounds were somber and inaudible. When Mamá came in she said the wedding will take place next Sunday if she could arrange it. And she did.

~ ~ ~

Standing by the wall of our house I held Juanito's hand and stared down at the styrofoam cup full of beer that someone had left in the grass near my foot. "How do you feel little one?" Uncle Jo asked me.

I heard the accordions beating a polka, and some old ladies exclaiming over the tamales and rice but I didn't hear Uncle Jo, not at first. No one, no grownup, had ever asked me that. "How do I feel about what?" I looked up at Uncle Jo and couldn't help but see how truly handsome he was.

"About your sister getting married? Te gusta?"

"It's OK," I finally answered. "I'll miss her and Papá wants her to stay at home."

"I know," he said. "Your Papá feels responsible for all of us, everything that we do. That's the way he was when we were little kids the same ages as you and Juanito. Whenever your Uncle Rudy and I got in trouble your Papá would always take the blame. Before he went to the war when none of us could find work, he drove all six of us brothers across the country looking for jobs. We didn't have a home. All of us were just kids, even him, only sixteen. But then he never seemed like a kid really. Did you know that about your Papá?"

"No, I didn't know that."
"Well, he never talks much about himself. But he and his family are surrounded by magic. Even I have seen the angels watching over your home. So don't worry. You are protected. Will you dance with me?"

Looking down at my shoes I mumbled, "I can't dance. I better not." And I watched him as he made his way over to my cousin and out on the dance floor.

Everyone got drunk at Cecilia's wedding. People whispered, "You know why she is marrying him. He..."

And my parents stood close, my mother smiling and speaking loudly. "Our daughter is so happy. He makes good money at the restaurant and he's already been promised a job as a truck driver for the meat packing company. Soon he will be in charge."

The men wore suits and cowboy hats and held the women tightly around their waists. Up in the sky I could see the sun, a big playful yellow tennis ball that changed in seconds to an orange beach ball like the ones Cecilia and I used to toss to each other on the beach in Corpus Christi. That beach ball just kept growing brighter and brighter until it was the brightest orangest ball I ever saw. It lowered itself behind our old tin shed where Papá keeps the tools, casting its red light on it so that the whole thing sparkled silvery red, glowing alive. The sky behind the sun darkened to purple and Papá stood stiffly at the back door waiting, his arm crooked at the elbow just a little and his eyes looking straight ahead at the magic light of the tool shed like maybe it would give him the spark he needed to begin.

Cecilia, wearing her beautiful antique white wedding dress, the one that Hector had bought for her not long ago, put her arm in his. Papá didn't look at her. He just stepped forward towards the two trees of our backyard, Antonio standing between them and the silvery tin shed on his right.

The leaves from the maple tree, gold and green fell in little swirls. Lights, like necklaces draped from tree to tree to clothesline to tree again, shimmering jewels in the purple dark. The white tablecloths from the picnic tables rippled with wind, the sound of wings flapping. I gave Papá a little smile as they passed me but he just kept looking straight ahead, no expression on his face. When he left Cecilia with Antonio, I thought I saw him glance over at her one last time but I can't be sure. Maybe I imagined it.

Aunt Irma behind me whispered, "Look how scared he is. He certainly does realize the seriousness of the occasion." She was talking about Antonio and sure enough from where I stood just a few feet away I could even see his knees shaking and him rocking back and forth on his heels. He looked at Cecilia shyly when she said she would love and honor him. And he almost put the ring on the wrong finger, but then he caught himself. "So sorry. So sorry Cecilia," he whispered.

She and Antonio had danced the first dance of the night. They twirled by me, their heads tilted back laughing. When that first dance was over Antonio yelled up in the sky, "I love you, Cecilia."

Everybody loves Cecilia. She blew him a kiss and danced on to a new partner, gaily collecting dollars to begin their marriage.

I walked around the house to look for the angels. I had heard about them so many times. They were large, about as big as the pecan tree out front, the one that touched the eaves of the house, and they were all golden except for their white gauze gowns. They had wings of course, and my mother had said they were surrounded by stars. Sometimes they sat on the roof. I didn't find the angels but I did find Papá who had managed to escape from the party and was sitting on the front porch with Ringo our cat sitting in his lap. I stood in the shadows of the lights hanging from the trees as he stroked the cat behind its ears and whispered the Hail Mary over and over again.

"Papá, where are the angels?" I asked him shyly.

"The wind carried one up there, over the Garcia's house. Tonight Maria's mother will have her baby and she needs our angel more than we do."

"Where?" I looked in the direction of the Garcia's house but only saw tree limbs swaying over the roof.

"The angel is in that Chinaberry tree, on the limb that falls near Maria's bedroom window." I looked again but saw no angel.

"What, you can't see the angel? But everyone in this family can see the angel."

I squinched up my eyes and looked as hard as I could but still I couldn't see anything.

"Well, no matter. The angels will always be near. The rest are in Cecilia tonight. She needs them to strengthen her marriage."

The next day Juanito and I had to climb the trees and unravel the strings of colored paper.

Mamá gathered litter from the picnic tables, sobbing quietly to herself, "It will never be the same again without her here. I know he will take her to Mexico and I will never see her again. She's gone, gone."

Papá stood in the middle of the trampled dusty grass of our back yard and announced to the empty chairs and to Mamá who refused to see him that Cecilia would never be able to have children and it would be for this reason that her husband would leave her. She would come home soon, but he would not accept her. He took his position on the front porch.

Later in the afternoon, Maria's mother stopped by. "Touch him, my new baby, so that he will have good fortune." With great flourish my Papá lightly swept his fingers across the infant's forehead. Then she left, satisfied. Papá never did come inside.

I wondered where the angels went in the daylight. Were they up here with me, invisible on a tree limb? How could Cecilia stand to make our parents so unhappy? I talked to the angel nearest me. "Please don't let me become like Cecilia. I will not be like my sister. I will stay here with Papá forever."

En Busca de los Niños

Antonia Quintana Pigno

> *It was the devious-cruising Rachel, that in her*
> *retracing search after the missing children, only*
> *found another orphan.*
>
> Herman Melville
> Epilogue, <u>Moby Dick</u>

I

There is a moment in the sand
     where all that follows
          must follow concentric lines
of wind upon the desert

where blood from five bullet wounds
     spreads away in hot sand and
          darkens each scene
that follows

where the great river cuts through the granite
     of the high mountain in its descent
          through the atomic city
          through desert valley

          and it is nothing
          nothing to the young husband
     who leans spent against the blue pickup
the spent heat of a gun in his hand

where the dead are collected beneath the dark moon
       and children fished from conservation ditches
            with brown and golden curls glistening
are borne into the night

where mothers veiled in anguish
       have lost their sons and having
       neither light nor language to understand
gather in sacred ritual of incense and adobe

where a father reminds his last
       and most lovely son that
           he is good   only good
for two things

where deep   deep   deep
       in the turquoise valley
           a mother lies in troubled sleep
restless until sons return

and where framed in the window of the distant Heights
       the slight girl in the white cotton slip
           is all there is
in the obsidian night

II

The child wedges into the space
between the window and heater
reading even as the sun lowers and
shadow darkens the page

A child is hiding in the tires
stacked along the east side of the house
he has run away and now waits
to be found   his legs tire

An infant cries at la tía
who has come to praise him with
the *mal de ojo* but there are eight
children and the mother turns first
here then there and the tortilla
is burning and the chile is burning
the frijoles need water and la tía
is laughing and the baby is crying and
the mother is crying

The mother is at peace in this dream
of incense and incantation
Lent and Fridays and the torturous
Stations of the Cross   Jesus
cries silent tears of blood   the mother
cries silently too   her black shawled head
bent for this Son whose burdened
journey takes sin away

In the Lenten pall the children suddenly remember
their mother is gone   and all
stop their play
listless and lonely

they sit on the porch
without past or tomorrow

Frijoles are not simmering on the stove
the smells of alien tortillas and chile
in the air all the way to the playing
field does not draw them into the holy dusk

III

You do not need speech anymore
and keep to yourself
Still you are young so there is beauty
in it   in your innocence
for madness made you so
you were borne into silence and such
silence forgets us and brings us alone
into this grief

your father fairly burst with it

Of man and woman
what were you to know and understand
all man and woman that you needed
by your cradle were gone
and the only lullaby you knew
was the thin blade of the moon song

you were borne into silence and such
silence forgets us and brings us alone
into this grief

your father fairly burst with it

Your mother was a pretty thing
her mind quick and a slender lily
amongst smaller and darker beings
and she was loved as only
the son loves the mother

you were borne into silence and such
silence forgets us and brings us
alone into grief

your father fairly burst with it

IV

juan ramón
could never
get those lines
straight why he used
his grandfathers name
and not his fathers
who was dead
and his mother was dead
and later his grandmother died
but the one he called *buelita*
called him *mijito*
and said he resembled his father
in his green eyes
and curly black hair
and his mothers father said
he resembled no one
and hated those eyes
and the curl of his hair
and everyone said his older brother chris

looked exactly like his mother
and chris would say
that in september he was
going to study ee at unm and
moments later he was going to
ohio to work construction in the
fall and his little brother memo
kept running away and so much
was said and happened that
juan ramón couldnt keep it
straight and so like barbed wire
it wound tightly around making
small wounds inside his head
that could never it seemed be
straightened out again

V

For Christmas
she gives gallon jars
of homemade pickles
labeled with Christmas seals
she wraps presents
with patches of brown bags
newspaper and foil
She mails packages
of cookie crumbs to nephews
just across the river
She wears smock dresses
belted at the waist—
bargains from rummage sales

She giggles shyly
as she cross examines
newly blushing girls
She bore a palsied son
who ate green grass until he died
he was five

VI

Joseph   Joseph Joseph
and where is your brightly colored coat
and where are your brothers
and where is your soft straw bed?
Your father lies in the red earth
these many years north of this sun
and your mother is also dead

You roam these white streets
and this same sun shines on you
that once made you break with smiles
but it is all the same to you
these days lead to death
and you have come to expect it

Your mother was a wild beauty
with cascading black curls
and her skin white as desert afternoon
laughter danced in her large and lovely
eyes and maddened your father's blood
rancored his green eyes

Passion burned them away from you
from your brothers

even before you learned to walk alone
and you are only dull ash left behind
to scatter through these bleak March streets
until the pauper's grave is rightfully yours
and lime the only white you draw about you

and tumbleweeds destined to wander
rest briefly there their dragging roots
until it is March again and sharp sand
and wind howl through deserted streets

VII

Today I weep for all the deaths
Today I weep for all the deaths
Today I weep for all the deaths
Come my love and kiss my tears

My father lies in a grave of yellow grass
my brother lies in a grave where grass shines green
my old aunt lies lonely for her grandsons
in a cold mountain grave

Your Ramanujan loved numbers and
left his beloved India to travel to chilly
England where still he loved numbers
but could not count on real ones after 32

The nine-year-old boy buried
in the high Andes
for 500 years has been found

and is beautiful still with his
braided black hair and wooden beads
and woolen cap and cape of many colors

In his day he brought great glory
to his brethren and to the Inca village
chosen as he was by the solemn grand priests
in their flowing white robes
for his was a virginal sweet smile
solemnly chosen to bring the sun's lordly
shine to the frozen reed air

My tears flow and I cannot check them
come, my love, and kiss me
kiss me

Today I think of all the deaths
and I am alone and far away
today the sky is gray through all
the cracks in the crumbling wall
and pine trees are heavy with rain
solemnly heavy with rain

and where is the boy whose golden smile
thawed the mighty sun
and where is my own love's warm
and moist kiss?

Today I weep for all the deaths
Today I weep for all the deaths
Today I weep for all the deaths
Come, my Lord, and kiss away my tears

THERE ARE BODIES in the desert. When I look through my lens, I see them clearly, but in bits—a stomach, a breast, a neck. The hill is a thigh, the shadow becomes a waist, the flat of the rock, the small of a back. I like to see this way, the parts that make the whole, one segment at a time.

I've been invited to this place by a woman I have known all my life. She offers me more than I realize in this invitation, she is passing something on, a gift, a secret. This is my first trip to the desert of southern Utah, and I find I am not prepared for the feelings I encounter. I was not warned that this will be a spiritual journey, that the desert will make sure of it and I quiver with inward excitement, a virgin, skin rising in tingles at each new sensation. I bring my camera, attempting to capture the memories as they happen, and the feelings. I quickly learn this will not be possible—the desert language showing itself word by word. I will have to wait, and listen.

In the desert, there is connection. I visit Delicate Arch and am moved by the way the arch envelops me, draws me to her, like a mother, like a siren, calling me home, to myself. Across from the womb-like bowl, a natural arena, she stands, a performer on a stage, or a god—demanding my reverence. I sit for hours just watching, and breathing her in.

~~~

We went to the Great Salt Lake to take pictures—the expanse a perfect backdrop for four naked dancing women. It took much coercing before they'd disrobe, each worried that her legs were the only with cellulite, or that her breasts were the only that had started to fall earthward.

We promised to let each frame be approved before any would be printed and assured them that the final print would be bleached and blurred so only faint nymph-like images are revealed. On the ground I found a bullet, corroded with time, but frighteningly new. A few feet away, there was an egg, or I thought it one until I felt it—it was a rock, in the perfect shape of an egg. I held these two, one in each hand, a bullet and a rock-egg, and said to myself, "here is a story, beginning and end."

A woman invited a man she'd met to share Thanksgiving dinner with her family. The man was from Mali, in Africa, and he talked a lot about his impressions of America. He told this woman that she was beautiful. He said that in his opinion, the women in America were too skinny, and this made them ugly, but that this woman was beautiful, because she was very large. He told her husband that her largeness was a sign of this husband's affection, that it was to his honor that she was big, because it proved that he made sure she had enough to eat. She was mortified by the African's comments. She blushed in front of her other guests. Later though, she felt angry that possible self-assurance was stolen from her. That there is a whole culture that would find her beautiful, but here, in her homeland of America, she had learned repulsion for her body.

I am thirteen and in eighth grade and am just learning that I look funny. Paul Kreason has informed me, in front of our biology group, that I don't need the bra I'm wearing. Red-faced, I smile, and look away. Later, I learn to joke about it first, so no one will think I care. At the beach, I am sixteen, and I am sure that the really nice boy I'm talking to would like me if I weren't so flat. At college winter break, I bring home the guy I've dated for five months. He's outside in the Jacuzzi, and I'm in the house just dying, because as soon as he sees me, he's gonna realize that I've been wearing thickly padded bras, that I've been lying.

When I was eighteen years old, I had augmentation mammoplasty, an operation to enlarge my breasts. It is 1985, and this is quite a common operation in America. My parents, with some hesitation, decide that since I feel so bad about my body it is worth fixing. I made my body my friend—I no longer despised it, or hid it under baggy clothes and slumped shoulders. Years later, I feign embarrassment among my "feminist" friends, for going under the knife, falling for the beauty rules I have been subjected to by men or society or whomever. But when I'm alone, I see my body and I feel like a woman, and I can't defend it perhaps, but I like feeling this anyway.

~ ~ ~

Everywhere I look, in many forms and dimensions, I see her, this ethereal desert woman. She is an arch, or an angry jutting rock, delicate and strong. I sit as the sun moves and she touches me, lightly crushing me in shadow dresses.

I see these natural arches, smooth and heaving, like a woman. Part of the harshness around them, but they are not harsh. Strength is theirs and it is given to me. I am in wonder at the fertility that abides here, not green or lush or easy, but new and alive just the same. I am here to worship. With anxious reverence I swallow the experience in gulps. Surely this is God's Zen garden, and I am impatient for the peace it offers.

~ ~ ~

On Sunday I shot pictures of my brother's girlfriend. She stood against a backdrop of black sandy mounds, at the quarry in North Salt Lake, her naked skin white in the six O'clock sun. We felt foolish and uncomfortable and shy. She apologizes for the flaws she thinks her body has and I try to assure her that she looks perfect, like a painting. I tell her not to worry, since I am shooting in black and white, and the cellulite she complains about and the broken vessels she hides won't even show. Soon, she is dancing and giggling and leaping, and feeling perfect in the naughtiness of enjoying her nakedness.

I went to an exhibit called 'Invasion of Personal Space.' The photographer had taken pictures of people he met on the street, strangers, who let him stand twelve inches from their noses and shoot a picture. The photos were blown up to 16 x 20 inches and were displayed along a wall from youngest to eldest. When I look at these faces, I am amazed by the grace each person possesses, and these are not people I'd normally see this way. But in the pictures, so big and so close, I see the light in their eyes. They are perfect in their realness, and beautiful.

Sometimes people ask why I only shoot in black and white. There is something about eliminating color—something that this erasure develops. I think the absence of color makes the image stronger, lets its language through, creating a barrier or lifting a curtain somehow, allowing me to see the beauty within, and feel it. Flaws are the beautiful thing in a colorless picture, adding interest, and texture, and realness. Airbrushed perfection is so easy, and boring.

Tomorrow I will shoot pictures of my cousin. We have had it planned for months, just waiting until she is big enough, waiting until this miracle can be clearly celebrated in a photograph. She says she is tired and uncomfortable. Her husband, she tells me, worships her largeness with caresses. He calls her the moon, a title she visibly loves. I think about her, this amazing ability she possesses, bringing life to this world. She contains everything this human-in-the-making desires. She needs no one to complete this task. She looks at her body and sees it clearly, not as an object to be dieted away, tucked and pulled, shunned. She sees it as a heavenly masterpiece, an instrument of unsurpassable functionality.

~ ~ ~

The night becomes, and I watch its making. First only scattered stars— I look again and see that thousands more have rushed to greet them, and me. I lie on my back, underneath, watching the silence, my skin full of starlight magic. Out here is an ocean of light, shimmering, like columbine in the wind. I wish I could say "Cassiopeia looks brilliant tonight" or "that one is called Orion," but those are the classes I never paid attention to, fleeing from their science into the galaxy of my imagination. Above me are clusters of tiny diamond worlds, tossed in random onto a rich black swath of velvet.

I dream. Placing my clothes on a blood-red rock, I walk to the edge of this mountain. There, I command the heavens, as conductor, and they respond in twinkling melody. The sacrament of the sky unfolds before me, and I partake. My cousin is there, round in her eighth month. I look in wonder at the way she is changed. Her body is amazing and beautiful and glorious. I lay my head on her stomach and hear the beating heart. I see my mother as she burns with the pain of birth, giving the earth its life, its breath. I watch her shape the mountains, the rivers, the rock and dune. In love I am engulfed by this desert body.

Daylight. I run the fingers of my mind over the body of this desert, caressing her. I admire the sculptor's gentle touch, the erosion that has shaped this perfect creature. The heat makes me dizzy and I move in search of a kinder sky. I find the crevice of two towering rocks. I wedge myself between, and standing, I press my face on the rock, and soak up its coolness. I listen to its pulse. I am not surprised by the comfort of this refreshment. I look out into the expanse, from the safety of my dwelling, and understand what this place is offering.

~ ~ ~

There is much to see in photographs of the bodies of women. They are each so different and so soft. When we go to the bookstore, I head straight for the photography books like I always do, and this time, I see the female body in the landscape of the desert. There is a book on the shelf, and on its cover is the stomach of a woman. I take a closer look because the title says something about landscapes and doesn't seem to coincide with the picture. It is a photograph of sand dunes in a desert.

When I look at myself, I want to see like a photographer. I want to see my body, the way it has changed and softened, and see the naturalness of time instead of the flaws of age. I want to view each imperfection as the desert landscape, in its glory, not easily given in a glance, yet beautiful in its rigidity, and necessary. I want to enjoy the wisdom purchased with these wrinkles, and accept the greying of my roots as earned beauty, a reward for the passage of time. I want to see this erosion as the necessary tool that, like weathering to the smoothed curves of the slick rock, holds inside, and releases, an astonishing kind of grace.

I once believed the desert was a dead and barren place, and cannot defend this prior blindness. If you look correctly, there is an abundance here that surrounds. Now I see the message clearly—love all of my parts, find the lushness in this seemingly empty place, see the individual pieces that make up this perfect and confusing whole, and embrace them. Our bodies are this desert—soft and hard, strong and vulnerable, anger and peace. My breath is the changing wind, my heart beats the pulse of the sun. The desert is calling. Answer.

View From the Deck

Emilie Vardaman

EARLY LIGHT softened the San Pedro Valley. The hills began to glow, making the sides of the mountains appear silky smooth. Even cholla and prickly pear seemed like a child's velveteen toy.

I watched the sun poke through splotchy clouds, early morning light softening the Huachuca Mountains to the west. Tiny beams of sunlight slipped through dense clouds hugging the tops of the Mules, changing colors on the western peaks from brown to rose to green.

The sun climbed and clouds began to wisp away. I took my breakfast out on the deck to watch the day come alive. Butterflies and hummingbirds joined me, searching out their breakfasts. The neighbor's cattle, accustomed to open range, brayed and moaned on the other side of the fence we'd erected to protect our home. They were sure the best grasses, leaves and mesquite beans lay just inside the barbed wire.

Two weeks until fall equinox, I'm preparing to begin my fiftieth year. I'm settling into my first year of life on our land in the desert.

I sat, eating a good-for-me breakfast and felt slightly like a TV commercial. Middle aged woman, smiling at the new day, enjoying healthy cereal. Cut to box...back to woman...fade as gentle wind blows hair across her face...

But it's not quite the same as a TV commercial, not yet. I wasn't perched on a deck railing or relaxing in a lawn chair. The deck has no railing and I have no chair.

The deck, only 5'x7', is attached not to a house or vacation cabin, but to a 23-foot school bus turned church bus. Its white color is faded and the name of the church has been painted over, but the words "Naco, AZ" remain lettered in turquoise. This is my new home.

I don't remember, as a child, what I thought life would be like as a grown-up. I played with dolls, but more often with my interlocking blocks and little plastic horses and cowboys. I built ranches, and over and over again played out the scenarios of ranch life.

Now, here I am, on my own small ranch, not yet clear where this new life will take me. I have no horse and no plan to get one. A mule would be more like it; a friendly beast to help me haul untold numbers of rocks out of the wash. Rocks for foundation, rocks for the stem wall, rocks for posts. I will build my house of blocks, just as I did as a child, but these blocks will be made of straw.

I thought about the rocks, the cement that needed mixing, the over-whelming amount of work facing me the next few years. My range of emotions throughout the day was like the range of light and shadow on the desert. The mountains moved from their early morning colors into green, then into blue as evening approached. My emotions moved from peace to frustration through despair and into acceptance.

I gazed out at San José Peak to the south, just across the line in Mexico. I thought about how the border had changed over the years, from a friendly place, where a few of the border guards were even amiable. Twenty years ago, I crossed weekly, at least, to shop, eat in one of many tiny living room restaurants, or drink in one of the whorehouses at the end of town. Crossing was easy and friendly, and I knew several of the guards by first name.

Today there is a wall, not a fence of holes where kids crossed daily to play with cousins and friends. The US Army spent months erecting this barrier to keep illegals and undesirables from entering our free country. The 10-foot steel wall runs a few miles in either direction of the crossing, and can be seen miles away, an ugly scar on the desert.

Here on my deck, the gentle hills to the south hide the steel line from view. From my deck, it appears that life is still kind, the border guards still friendly, and that no walls divide families or interrupt children at play. The view from my deck gives me the energy and the heart to face the rocks and cement, to begin the foundation of my new life.

A Chant for Remembrance

Elizabeth Ann Galligan

Let her return to the earth today
to this shallow, open basin
cupped only by sky and mountain

above and all around

Let her return to the earth today
to the Mother honored by her children
in pattern, song and story

below and all around

Let her return to the land today
adopted daughter of Anasazi
sister to the Athabascan

to the east and all around

Let her return to the land today
passing harmoniously
into role of ancestor

to the south and all around

Let her return to the earth today
who studied paths of people
carrying culture in their hands

to the west and all around

Let her return to the earth today
ringed by sacred mountains
merging into memory

to the north and all around

Let her return to the earth today
her sand-painted patterned life
one with the earth at dawn.

In fond and respectful memory of Bertha Pauline Dutton, mentor and guide, somewhere in the Galisteo Basin of New Mexico, returned to her beloved land, September 23, 1995.

The Bad Egg

Sherry Luna

The jar of pickled eggs sits there week after week
perched on the wooden headboard.
Abuelita put them up fresh when the old man got sick—
lung cancer and kidneys, Camels and mescal—
but now they look yellow and rubbery,
like if you drop them they'll bounce.
You can buy pickled eggs at Leon's Market for fifty cents,
but those eggs are for eating.
These eggs draw poisons and evil spirits
from the old man's body—
a pagan version of transference.
Through the smell of urine and disinfectant
comes the scent of rotting flesh.
If you avoid looking at the decaying old man,
you can pretend the odor comes from the eggs.
If you cave in to your true feelings,
you can gloat over the truth.

But the huge crucifix nailed over the bed prohibits this
so you turn your attention to that instead
and peering through the dust motes you count the drops of blood
on Christ's face.
Abuela never leaves things to chance
even though she's fond of saying,
"You've got to have faith, *mija*"
and is a devout bingo player.

The soldiers offered Christ vinegar rather than water
and laughed when he turned his face away.

In Zacatecas Abuela was a *curandera*, a healer,
and people brought her their sick and lame along with a chicken.
Catholicism in the States changed this somewhat.
The hexes and frogs and roosters disappeared
but the rue for menstruation,
deer blood and bull testicles for virility,
and, of course, the eggs remained.
Christ had *huevos* but didn't come from an egg.
Maybe that's the connection:
the miracle of the egg, the eggless miracle.

Easter Sunday after Mass the family always hunted eggs
dyed with colored vinegar water.
Symbols, the priest said, of the resurrection.
Except one always got lost...
until its smell revealed the ultimate ephemerance of symbols.
Did the old religions ask so much of their gods?
This well-preserved cycle of death and redemption?
You think not—remembering stories
of the Virgin Huntress swollen and fertile,
pulling the Horned One forth onto the yielding earth
and the circle of egg and blood forming a living ritual
for the renewal of life...

This old man gave you life through *his* son
but you stand there steeped in memories as bitter
and well-preserved as eggs suspended in vinegar
and the weekly visitation seems as barren
as that long, hungry journey through confession...

You think of many things in the room of a dying man
and most will not make sense
like an egg suspended in vinegar and a god hung on a cross.

Salt River

Laura Tohe

In the hands of the river
    she caresses them
        into shapes of her thoughts

In the hands of the river
  she cradles them, her children
        filled with splendid dreams of rushing water

In the hands of the river
    she forms them into language
    calls them beloved

In the hands of the river
    she reaches for the touch of the sky
        who colors their faces with pink and lavender sunsets
         and sprinkles their bodies with stars

In the hands of the river
    she nurses them into rounded shapes like bread,
        earth people whose bodies have risen from the earth
         released from the song of their mother's belly
         and offers them to this world

Believe this,
Believe in the hands of the river

The Grand Canyon

Judith McDaniel

...have faith in me
I am the world's smallest traveling altar.
I am the altar and its door,
The prayer and the yearning—

Marilyn Chin
"The Narrow Roads of Oku"

The Rim

We travel for a long time toward this place
across the blackened volcanic hills
through scrub pine holding to bedrock
under the narrow dirt
past scraps of snow lingering on tundra.

And then it comes so suddenly,
the blink of an eye, one last step toward the edge
and we are staring down at all creation, the depths
out of which all life
the source
the beginning.

I stand astonished,
shaken at the raw and vulnerable rock
yawning awake before me.

Climbing Down

In the first hour of the descent
the lower legs take the strain,
the calves begin to ache

—anticipation of nine more hours
climbing downward. The second hour
is slower, even the pain

moves up the thighs more slowly.
Gripping at rock through leather soles
burns my toes. In the fifth hour

we begin the Cathedral Stairs—

winding north, then south, on switchbacks
tortured out of rock fissures,

stepping down one rock, then another,
heading at one moment directly back,
it seems, to where we began
only a few yards lower. Now my legs
tremble to the bone when I stop moving.

I pause to look back and up
and realize I have descended
into the cathedral. Above me rise
the spires of what is possible beyond imagining—
lava cooled as it shot out of the earth,
pressed into permanence.

After the switchbacks a long path moves straight down
the talus slope. I walk on, past flowering cactus
and purple sage, small wildflowers in the cranny of rock,

down and down to the river. We have
been climbing down for nine hours.

Have you ever 'hit the wall' in your running?
my friend asks. I haven't. I know I've never pushed
that hard. Today I hit it over and over,
imagine each time I am smashing
into my absolute physical limit,
but I cannot stop this descent

and so I go on.

The Wall

We sit under a ledge while the rain seeps into our skin
from the rock behind our backs. My hair has been wet
for two days and my fingers are washtub wrinkled.

Surrounded by rock I stare hard at the canyon wall,
looking for patterns, directions. Monsters
stare back from the dripped lava mud and canyon squirrels

flit in and out of caves, finding impossible perches
on edges of nothing. On the rim a stone eagle rises
toward flight and—as I stare—a dinosaur with open mouth

lurches from the rock. A million years of activity
carve that rough wall. Hour after hour
I sit silent, let the noise within

merge with the canyon wind and the spiral fall
of the canyon wren's call and the drip of mist
as it becomes a rocky stream. I look

into the wall's ancient cipher and see
myself. I am alone.
No companionship could breach these walls.

Here. Now. My shoulder leaning into this wall
is deception, the wall is my shoulder, my hand is
the wall which builds walls around me, smooths wetness

into my stone lungs, hardens my lava mud skin.
How should I ever dream that I could share
the breath of a star or feel on this rockface

the canyon wren's feather fall? There is terror
in the finality of a body. It is what it is,
as the rock is not the squirrel, so with each

succeeding age we have lost a bit of that
which bound us together, allowed our edges
to merge, leaving only that last miracle—

birth—which binds our form until death.
The return seems impossible: to dismantle
rock by rock this terrible finality, alter

this lonely individuality, believe that I
could stare into the wren's dark eye until I fall,
lost, into her depths.

Coming Back Out

We sit under that ledge for a day
and a night and when the black drizzle

greys, we pack up and start
the climb out. My friend says

the key is our pace and she leads us
slowly, our footsteps steady as

heartbeats. Packs weighing
like the world above us press down

on our backs. I try not to look up
not to imagine the nine miles ahead

our destination hidden in the mist
and clouds above. For the first hour

I am sure the climb out is not
possible. My feet are bruised and raw

and the pack straps cut my shoulders
with the weight of seven days uneaten food,

a sleeping bag sodden with rain.
One foot, then the other. Eyes cast down,

I watch the pattern of rock beneath,
wonder at the glow of cactus flowers

in the icy sleet, the grey light.
Suddenly we turn around a rock ledge

and find three boys huddled under one
rain poncho. I want to walk on,

keep my focus on putting one foot ahead
of the other, but we stop, ask *what's wrong?*

Oh, he's tired, says he can't make it,
so we're going to leave him here and go
get our leader to come back for him.
And my pack strap broke so I'm gonna leave
my pack here too. We'll be back,
one assures us, then they head off. The boy
under the poncho shivers, smiles with some
embarrassment at his own weakness. I look
more closely and see the blue shadow
under the line of his lips, the tremor
shaking out from his body core. *Where*
is the leader who is coming back for you?
I want to know. *Up there.* He nods toward
the rim and wraps his arms around his chest
to hold the shaking. *The guys said they'd*
send a ranger in a helicopter for me,
that's what they do when people get stuck.

I have had the same fantasy this morning
so I try to be gentle as I tell him
to look at the fog swirling down, rolling
along the grass, wrapping itself around rock
faces and smothering the light. *My dad's*
the leader, he assures me, *he'll make*
the rangers come and get me. I am
angry now, angry at the interruption of my
meditation, the quiet repetition of step
upon step that was making the climb out
seem possible, angry at a leader who would

leave any child shivering in a wet t-shirt,
angry at this child who believes the impossible.
You're going to walk with us, we tell him
and pull out sweaters, dry socks, a candy
bar, and canteens of gatorade. He stumbles
for a while, his toes falling lower than
his heel, but gradually he recovers,
fed, warmed, accompanied, and bounds ahead
on the path, chattering, while I still plod,
placing one foot heavily in front of the other.

In the Morning

I walk back out across the rim
staring down as a shaft of sunlight
tries to pierce the heavy clouds beneath.

Today I am looking down
at a place where I have been.

I have climbed in
and back out.

In late spring we expected
seven days like this morning on the rim—
hot sun, a desert landscape
where water would be scarce.

We weighed each ounce of food and gear,
judged what was necessary,
what weight we could bear,
what could be discarded.

And yet we were unprepared. Rain,
then unexpected snow, overtook us.
We carried baggage we didn't need,
left behind gear we longed for.

Beneath me the canyon is silent,
covered in a dreamer's cloud swirl.
A puff of occasional wind moves the mist
in waves of thought.

I have lost friends and lovers,
lost children not of my blood and the parents
whose blood gave me this life. I have shed
pieces of myself as I walked across the landscape
toward this place,
shed the ways in which I knew myself:
names and work and place, none stood by,
and yet
something remains that was with me from the first
some impulse, some stance, some way of beginning
that roots this life against the precipice,
that curls—a tight-fisted seed—waiting,
always waiting for the fire's clean sweep.

The Good Daughter
Rita Garitano

To HONOR my Mama, I made my weekly visit home. She sat at the kitchen table. Wearing her old chenille bathrobe, she'd been moving about, trying to come back to life, but her skin was the color of adobe washed with lime. I asked, "Shouldn't you be resting?" She looked at me with infinitely tired eyes as if I were a cat yowling for food when she had none to give. I'd forgotten how hopeless I felt when I couldn't ease her pain. I stood by the table, fidgeting, "Can I bring you more coffee?"

She shook her head "no." And then to show me how foolish my offer was, how she really didn't need me, she touched a cup of coffee to her lips and sipped. Setting the half-empty cup on the table, she fluttered her fingers about the rim while she waited for me to leave.

I glanced at the cupboard and the enamel kettle on the stove. "Has Aunt Megda brought more food?" My family has never gone hungry. Mama would never understand my self-imposed starvation.

Her face was impassive as she said, "There's only your father and me to eat all that food." She looked at the old chair where I used to sit to have my hair braided. Every morning, she'd pulled my hair so taut I whimpered, then she scolded, *"If I don't pull it tight, all your wild curls will spring up and get away."* I sat in that chair to do all my lessons to make my Mama proud of her girl who earned A's. I sat in that chair when I cleaned my plate. In high school, I was banished from that chair, sent to wash off my lipstick and rouge and mascara before I was allowed to leave the house.

I murmured, "So there's nothing I can cook for you?" And, of course, we both knew the answer. I don't cook. When Megda and Kamela and Mama spent days at cooking, I dallied on the fringe of their circle, never doing a thing unless they ordered me to, and then being so clumsy that Megda sneered, *"She may be a smart girl, but she don't know nothing about cooking."* I was Cinderella, who served Megda and Mama and cleaned up the kitchen.

Mama sat at the table so silently, so lost in some thought of the past, I spoke softly so I wouldn't disturb the deep stillness where she floated. I asked, "Mama, could I wash your hair?" I was surprised by my offer, for it'd been ten years since we had washed one another's hair. I hoped she wouldn't be angered by my request, one I was sure she'd reject.

She tilted her head slightly as if she might be remembering our weekly ritual. Saturday evenings, all through my years in grade school, and even junior high, we washed our hair. With dozens of hair pins removed, the coil of Mama's hair unwound and fell in a mane so thick and alive, the kitchen sink seemed filled with a bolt of unwound silk. With her head poised over the sink, her eyes closed, I worked above her, careful not to let our bodies brush, as my fingers kneaded from the scalp down the strands until the acres of hair were lathered. I rinsed and rinsed and rinsed until the hair squeaked with cleanliness. Then with the turban of the towel about her head, Mama washed my hair. Even when Mama was younger, her breasts and belly were ponderous. Their soft warmth brushed against me, again and again, so I was bathed in the smell and touch of her as she toiled. After she bound my head tightly in a towel, I'd release her turban and begin to comb, gently working through the mass of tangles until hair hung past her shoulders and dried in swirls of waves. With hair pins in her teeth, Mama reached behind her head and wrestled her hair, compressing all the life into a hard ball at the nape of her neck. Stabbing the pins into place, she hid the beauty of her hair until the next week.

Not looking at me, Mama spoke to herself, "Yes, I'd like my hair washed."

"Now? You'd like to have it washed now?" This woman I could never please was asking me to serve her. To touch her was frightening.

She didn't look up, but nodded as if she counted beads as she murmured prayers of the Rosary.

"Just tell me where the shampoo is and the towels—" And I knew as I said it they'd be where they've always been; the objects of this house are as unchanging as the rocks of the Catalina mountains.

She hobbled to the chair that I'd placed with its back to the sink and took her place. With her eyes closed, she laid back her head. Her upturned face was poised so rigidly, her neck must have pained her. Beneath her flickering eyelids, she might've been imagining what I'd remembered. Maybe she was as frightened as I was, as starved for touch. I slipped my hands beneath her neck. As I eased her head onto the towel to cushion against the cold enamel, the weight of her tension was numbing. With both hands free, I brushed my fingers through strands of white and silver and grey and an occasional hair of the deepest black. Age had thinned the dense hair, and the absence of color changed the texture. Now her white hairs were the strongest and most plentiful, as thick and resilient as the nylon of Papa's fishing line. I was saddened by the memory of her luxuriant, wavy hair, so black it was blue in the sun.

Since Papa hasn't fixed the water heater, it flows hot or cold. I let the water from the faucet drip on my wrist to test the heat like a baby's formula. Then I turned up the force, so tepid water cascaded over the forest of hair and streamed over her temples. I splayed my fingers to open spaces so the water poured through, matting the strands, which I rubbed against one another, again and again until they were limp with water.

Beneath the wet band of silver hair, Mama's face was grey. The cold shampoo had to be carefully applied about the roots of the hair at the forehead and worked down to the ends of the strands tangled in the sink. She waited, her heavy hair pulling her head back, so the tendons on her neck stood up like ropes. To warn her, I murmured, "Ready?" before I touched the shampoo to her temples. Massaging my hands through her hair, I reached further and further into the sink. Some strands of hair were two feet long, maybe two and a half. If hair really grows half an inch a month, the growth by her scalp was hair I'd never touched since our days of mutual grooming. My body hovered so close to her, her breath glanced from my arm. Everywhere we touched, her steady, labored breathing moved through me.

My fingers and hands ached after the first massage, and still I must rinse, pouring cup after cup of water over and through the strands to wash all the suds away. And then the shampoo and rinse must be repeated again. How totally harmless Mama seemed, lying waiting for the first rinse to begin, this woman I had given such power, this woman I'd quoted, "*My mother says, my mother thinks, my mother believes.*" She looked so vulnerable, so very human, tears sprang to my eyes, but I bit my lip for control. I must care for her, take care to be a good mother to my mother. My voice sounded reassuring as I said, "We're almost halfway there." Mama's lips tightened as though she willed herself to suffer longer. How terrified she must have been when I became a girl who defied her mother, this woman who fears everything she can't control. I'd be a decent daughter. I'd finish Mama's shampoo with the gentle touch and soothing manner of the good mother.

Mama's eyes were closed. She was so still that she might've been sleeping. For the last cycle of the shampoo, I must be thorough; I had to be careful to cleanse each strand. When I was a child, Mama always told me, "*You must work hard and care for your beautiful hair. Your hair is your crowning glory. A very wealthy man might want a wife with such beautiful hair.*" So I'd been a good daughter, stoically enduring Mama's powerful hands kneading my scalp until it throbbed, until the shampoo billowed. And even when my tightly closed eyes teared, I hadn't complained. I'd never whined when the water was too hot or too cold or if it ran into my ears. My neck and my shoulders and back were taut with my efforts to be a good daughter, so beautifully groomed that I might be chosen to marry a wealthy man, a very wealthy man. I worked my fingers gently into Mama's hair. I didn't scold as she did, or endlessly explain how everything must be done perfectly. My fingertips did not dip into her scalp with such pressure that it was almost pain. My hands glided through the twisting river of hair. I wouldn't stop until every strand was clean.

I touched the fraying chenille covering Mama's shoulder and asked if she'd like to rest a few moments. The last rinse must be perfect, for Mama once warned, "*Unless every bit of shampoo is rinsed away, your hair won't be perfect. It will be dull. It will be just as dirty as if you hadn't washed it.*" But Mama shook her head *no*, refusing to rest. She never voices her exhaustion as if it were a paper-thin communion wafer dissolving slowly on her tongue. My voice trembled as I said, "The last rinse might take some time. Maybe, a little rest would be good." But she dipped her chin *no* once. Her face was such a monument to a dutiful life. Perhaps she was preparing to leave her body. Perhaps she was planning to leave her terror of this world for a place she believes in, where at the end of her pilgrimage, she'll be with the saints and all her lost babies, with God and Jesus and the Holy Spirit.

To wash the shampoo from the long hair, I filled a chipped porcelain cup with water and slowly poured it over the tangles above the death mask of her face. This is the face Mama wore when she learned about my scholarship, my passport out of the Barrio. Frozen by my excitement, she stared into a pot of beans she stirred at the stove as I exclaimed, "Oh, Mama, Mama, I have a scholarship. I won a full scholarship to, to the University of Arizona." And she hadn't even lifted her eyes from the pot on the stove. She just nodded twice as if this confirmed her daughter would never be a wife down the block with babies to see every day, and now we would have even less to say to one another. The University, a place with such power, such beautiful gardens, and acres and acres of buildings, with students and professors, frightens Mama. On lazy Sunday afternoons when Uncle Rey took the family on drives to the center of town, to the University, the place for wealthy Anglos, Mama was so overwhelmed, she never even got out of the car to walk on the campus. She's never passed among the professors and students, everyone busy and so full of life. Mama did not come to the commencement of the first university graduate in the family.

I filled another cup and watched the water disappear in the steel grey. Even though I hadn't married at fifteen like Anna Ruiz or gotten pregnant in high school like all of Megda's girls, it didn't matter. Even though I'd earned all A's, a perfect record, the winner of the gold T at Tucson High; a Homecoming Princess, a popular girl; none of it mattered because Mama didn't understand. She couldn't share in the pride of winning a scholarship to the university to be a teacher. Teachers made twenty—*twenty*—five thousand dollars a year. Four times more than Papa. I'd have an education for a profession. I wouldn't be a graduate of Allure Beauty college, or Pima, but the University of Arizona. They wanted me: a scholarship to the University of Arizona.

A dozen more cups of water might rinse the suds away. Mama is so paradoxical; the more she suffers, the less she shows. Now, she was so still, so dusty grey, so cold, so decayed. So little life showed, she was the living dead. I have searched and searched through my memories of Mama to remember when she gave me a sign of warmth. As she fitted the red velvet formal for the senior prom when I was a princess, she said, "Gloria, you're beautiful." And even though I tried and tried and tried to win her approval, I can't remember it ever happening again. For she was always busy, always hovering over some quilt or something at the stove or sink. Always prayerfully silent at that sink, keeping her world clean, scouring an ancient aluminum pot until all its dents shone. She could never ever leave the house to come to the high school to see her daughter dance, not as a song leader. Even the sight of me in my uniform turned Mama's face away. As she pinned the hem to make the skirt shorter, with a row of pins sticking out of her lips, her eyes never left the yard stick. She was dressing her daughter for the streets. Her daughter, the *puta*, was going to flounce around in underpants in front of men and women and children. With little swats of the yardstick as a command, I turned so Mama would jab in the next pin. When she pulled the dress over my head, the pins pricked my arms. Angrily, she stitched the hem of a uniform so skimpy all of her daughter's body would show. And Alberto stood by me on the football field, his helmet shading his reptilian eyes. He said, "Girl," as he slipped his hand under my skirt, "you got the best legs on the squad. Forget about those Anglas. You're a woman," and he grabbed a fistful of flesh. Mama had not even come to see me perform as a lead dancer at Tucson High when I'd danced in seven dances from as classical as Bach to as modern as Martha Graham.

As water flowed through her hair, her eyelids fluttered as if she'd seen a vision. She would have been shocked if she'd seen her daughter, the song leader, naked as a centerfold girl, walk to the showers in the locker room, giggling and talking, with twenty-five girls with towels wound around their hair. Mama would never have understood the locker room, not even with her wonderful English, English she never forgot like the neighbor ladies had, some who went all the way through high school and haven't spoken English since. Mostly, the girls on the squad were Mexican, with a couple of blacks and Jess, who they called the Albino. Once one of the squad, a gangly black girl, looked at me and said loudly, "Hey, señorita, you got the sexiest body this side of the border. You got to drive the boys crazy." And Jess, who had the body of a twelve-year-old, just laughed, trotting up beside her friend, giggling, "Hey, Glo, it's true. Ask Alberto, right?" Oh, Mama, Jess thinks sex is funny. She talks about being horny as if she's hungry. Jess thinks *puta* is a funny word, turning it into a sixties rock song.

Six cups and still the pool floating over Mama's hair was watered milk, scuds of rain clouds over the Catalinas. She never came to the University, where football games were like the Roman Coliseum with gladiators suited up for blood. The swarm of football players on the field would have totally confused her; the song leaders' dances to blaring music were so sexual, she would have averted her eyes with shame. Dancing semi-nude as a song leader, I teased the fans with electric energy. A white cross cranked me up for show time. So Mama wasn't really needed. If she'd come, drugs would have been out and doing the routine straight would have been a drag. And Mama would have been paralyzed with embarrassment to meet the other parents. Jesse's mother, an elegant, Jewish matron, and her husband, a successful stock broker, would have totally intimidated Mama. She could never have climbed the concrete steps of the bleachers, for Papa was too frail to lean against. He'd probably have wandered off with Rey sipping from a bottle in a brown paper bag. And Papa would have gotten lost in the crowd of drunken Anglos pushing and shoving. He'd be glossy-eyed with terror, shoved up against a wall.

I finished the rinse and wrung out the tired hemp of her hair. She stoically stared ahead as I combed out the tangles and put her back together again. I knew I could never know what she feels, or what she's thinking—this mound of ashes who had frightened me so. I was sorry I couldn't do more for this woman who has survived all these years with her fear of love.

The Last Supper

Maria Leyba

MAMÁ'S ROLLING PIN going ta-tat-ta-tat-ta-tat was the very first sound Alma heard when she woke up. The smell of freshly made tortillas always lured her out of bed at dawn. What she loved best was hearing Mamá's beautiful harmonious voice. Always singing corridos while she worked in the kitchen, Mamá was a meadow-lark stuck in the desert of brown sparrows. This morning Mamá wasn't singing, nor did her rolling pin make its familiar sound. Alma heard only the nervous screech of the rolling pin going ta-tat-ta-tat-ta-tat.

The voices coming from the kitchen were strained and tight as if being pushed through a sieve. The concrete houses the state furnished for the workers at the New Mexico State Penitentiary were so compact: Alma only had to sit up in bed to hear her parents' conversation.

Papá's hurried voice said "Luisa, when will the extra tortillas be ready? I have to go to work soon. Please hurry."

Mamá's voice seemed lost as she answered, "I can't believe that the gringo wants to eat tortillas as part of his Last Supper."

"I know it sounds strange. All he asked for was tortillas, beans, red chili and papitas. Imagine, he could have asked for steak, or any first class food. That gringo wants to die with his stomach full of Mexican food," Papá answered wearily.

Mamá's voice faded as she asked, "What time is the execution?"

"It should be later in the evening. The executioner will be arriving from out of state later in the day. Only Warden Brown knows who he is. The executioner will wear a black mask the whole time he is at the penitentiary. Luisa, the prisoners are already in mourning for a fallen comrade. Since yesterday they have all refused to leave their cells," Papá patiently replied.

Papá was the head cook at the penitentiary. Several times Alma had gone with Papá inside the penitentiary. Fear mixed with curiosity compelled her to follow Papá's shadow into what she would later refer to as the devil's house. Papá proudly showed her off to everyone, as he took her on a personal tour stopping first at the gas chamber. The dark gray metal chamber had felt like ice, her tiny body quivered. The thought of someone sitting in the massive black chair with so many leather straps took her breath away. Papá showed her where he had stood to watch the last execution. He had even showed her the black lever the executioner pulled down to start the gas leaking.

Alma sat upright rocking back and forth in bed, struggling to understand why one of the prisoners in her backyard would have to die tonight. She couldn't remember getting dressed, and next thing she knew she was running from her house into the desolate llano. Alma collapsed on a little dust hill filled with yuccas, next to a barbed wire fence and a metal lean-to. Directly in front of her was the only road into Santa Fe. Maybe if she waited long enough the yellow school bus from the neighboring town of Cerrillos would rescue her. Take her in to town and find Father Green, he could stop the execution.

It was the middle of summer, and she crawled into the lean-to shading herself from the blazing desert heat. Fondly she remembered how the prisoners had built the metal lean-to that sheltered her from the cold winters, as she and her brothers along with eight neighboring children waited for the bus to take them to school in Santa Fe. In two months she would be starting third grade. Alma was so proud that she could finally speak English fairly well. The first two years of school had been so hard, never quite knowing what the teacher or the other children were saying. Every school morning she had left Mamá's Mexican kitchen headed straight for the metal lean-to. She thought she had heard voices rattling underneath it, urging her to go to school and be brave and patient. Each afternoon when she stepped off the bus, the lean-to seemed to welcome her home. Some of the prisoners would be outside cleaning the fields. Only Cochise, the Indian prisoner, dared to speak to her. He knew when the teachers and children had made fun of her Mexican name or laughed at her broken English. Alma loved looking into his slanted obsidian eyes set deep in his brown weathered face, where she saw only the reflection of her innocence wrapped in his compassion.

But it was Cochise's voice so gentle and soft that made her skin prickle. Sometimes Alma thought that she heard the wounded cries of a child rattling in his throat. She could still hear Cochise's voice talking to her.

"Alma, you are the one who will never forget who she is and where you come from. Never, never forget your people."

Tears streaked her face as her angry little hands pummeled the hard ground. Alma pleaded with God to stop the execution, knowing the bus would never come. She fell asleep dreaming that the vast brown llano swallowed up the entire penitentiary and dissolved it into little pieces. All the prisoners were transformed into newborn babies. Nurtured now by the underground loving mothers, when they grew up they were pushed back into this world where they lived peacefully, away from the walls of hell.

Paco found his nine-year old sister curled asleep inside the metal lean-to. Tenderly he woke her up and cradled her in his strong 10-year-old arms. He finally convinced her to come home.

As they walked hand in hand, Paco said, "Hermanita, why are you such a funny little girl. Why do you have to feel everyone's pain?"

Alma couldn't answer, all she could do was sob. All day she stayed in her room, on strike just like her friends at the penitentiary. After supper she could hear her brothers laughing as they watched television in the living room. Suddenly the lights went out, and they were immersed in total darkness for what seemed an eternity to Alma.

Papá's voice broke the silence as he sat in the kitchen with Mamá. Sadly he said, "It's over, he's gone."

The next morning Alma woke up feeling so numb, she just wanted to lay in bed. She pulled the sheets over her head desperately trying to drown out Mamá's voice and rolling pin. That darn bolillo back to its familiar ta-tat-ta-tat-ta-tat. It was a miracle that she heard the persistent tapping on her window. At the same time she felt a strange prickling sensation chill her body. Alma peeked through the sheets and saw a beautiful little white bird pecking at her window. Quickly she dressed and ran outside, attempting to catch the little bird. He flew across the desolate llano towards the penitentiary. Alma's little feet skimmed across the ground as she happily followed the little bird. Her little pet stopped next to a small pool of water underneath the prison walls. Alma wondered why she had never noticed this little pool. Little white flowers were growing in the middle of the pool, and Alma thought that they looked like little white ducks. She forgot all about the bird as she sat on her knees playing with the white ducks. She spent the whole morning pinching off the little flowers and letting them float in the water. Alma knew who had planted this little pool just for her. Never would she share her secret with anyone.

Salvage Yard

J. M. Kore Salvato

I WALK and walk to get down to the
double wide, past the cars without wheels, or fenders, or doors, with
parts of their innards missing, their hoods up in the air. The heat makes
everything shine—all this chrome on the cars shines. Even the air shines.
I can't get used to it. Not like the rain where I'm from. Larry and his
uncle laugh when I say it's hot. It's only May, they tell me. Silver is all I
see, a silver haze on all sides. It's full of promise here. You know how Cortez
must have felt, coming up on those golden cities of his, way down south.

I open a car door. I don't remember if I've checked this one out or not. I
have to be careful, feeling in these seats for change. So far I've cut my
hand on a knife, then on an old screwdriver. I found some gloves that I
wear now, since I heard about the scorpions down here. I find a lot of
pens, crayons, old tools, used condoms, some change, of course, which
keeps us all in cigarettes.

Five hundred cars. That's a lot of potential cigarettes. Take this car. It's
a rusted blue—something. Chevy Impala. I have to check the writing
on the glove compartment—I mean glove box; that's what they call it
down here.

I've got my own set of tools, thanks to Larry's uncle, after that big find.
Seven hundred bucks. Now I've got a big fat screwdriver to pry open
the glove compar—box. Like this one. The silver button's rusted shut.
Insert screwdriver along the side, pry that door off. Owner's manual,
toilet paper, a cardboard Marlboro box. Once I found some money
wadded up in a cigarette box.

I open it. Two cigarettes. Not what I had in mind. My luck hasn't been too good lately.

Larry gets a thrill out of my finds, the money anyway, at the end of the day. It was his idea to set me treasure hunting like this. His uncle—he owns the place—deals his junk cheap. Says his junk is spelled "junque" and his shit don't stink. Wasn't too sure about me staying on. A girl, how old? Fifteen? After I found the envelope in the glove box with the seven hundred, though, his uncle gave us the double wide way down at the other end of the lot. No running water or toilet, and a window's out, but that's all right. At least Larry got the electricity going for the television. We shower in the bathroom over at the office.

I light up one of the cigarettes. Stale as hell. I hear some talking. I look out over the dashboard.

Two old people. The man bends down, jiggles the exhaust pipe.
"Look, Henry," the woman says to him, which isn't too smart since he's looking underneath the car. She lifts her sunglasses up. Puts them down. "It's an old boneyard here, Henry. It gives me the creeps."

No way, lady, no way. I let my breath out, the smoke shining like everything else. It's silver; it's all shiny around here. Always something new. It's like a new city way down the road of time. Even more machines will be around. These cars already give you that feeling. When I'm old, really old, it'll be a lot of flash and shine. Like this. Shine rising up to the sky.

And new things. Take that diary I found yesterday. Now there was a find. Could have belonged to somebody important.

"Hey, Mary! Get your ass out of there. Uncle Jack and I gotta eat. Go watch the phones."
"Sure, okay. Fine, Larry."

They bring me back a taco from the Mexican fast food truck. I work a couple of cars pretty good in the afternoon, but I don't turn up anything.

I go back to the office. Larry and his uncle are getting ready to go out again. Now that Larry's twenty-one, they've been staying out late. His uncle's in the bathroom. His wife kicked him out a while back. She got the house and he moved into the office. He sleeps here; he's rigged up a Mr. Coffee, but that's about it.

"Get me a fake ID," I tell Larry.
"Goddamn it." His uncle hurries out. He slams his fat fist on the counter, his undershirt riding up over his hairy stomach. "No underage bitch, run off from some hell hole and I take her in, is getting my establishment in trouble with the *law*." He points out the door when he gets to 'the *law*.'

So it's another trek down to the double wide. A few daisy-looking things on the ground. This is wildflower season? And these cactuses do not look much better with a ring of flowers on their head. At least there's no rain. Sure, Seattle has real flowers, but who wants all that rain?

When I get to where I'm going, I sit down at the card table I found in the back of a truck. One good chair came with the trailer, along with this lamp made to look like a ship at the bottom.

I'm starved. I get up, light up my last cigarette, slide open the tiny kitchen window. Down past the property I catch sight of a small fire. Just the Mexicans.

The diary's still there, at the end of the table. It's been there all day. Larry thought I ought to throw it out. Didn't even tell his uncle I found it. Just like he didn't tell his uncle he met me at the Truck Stop Cafe. He told me he liked my bony ass and my long blonde hair. He told his uncle he met me at a soup kitchen, trying to make ends meet. That's funny, isn't it? I wouldn't be caught dead in one of those things. In

Seattle the food is lousy: brown rice and broccoli. Herb tea. So sixties. And store cookies. Give me a homemade cookie and I'll go.

I sit down, pull the diary over. The cover's missing. But there's a fine piece of leather at the back. Black binding, like a Bible. I touch the top corner where there's a triangle of paper. A lot of pages must have been torn out. Then the ink's very faded. The writing's only on one side of the page. Small, neat handwriting.

1 January 1975

Expansive mood tonight. Saw Moon in a dream. He salutes me, then takes me into the swamps with him, like it was the old days between us. "Shitty way you were offed, man," I tell him. "You cook dinner for the little bastard—you know, slip the pint-sized gook a little something when nobody's looking. The kid brings you a grenade for dessert."
Moon shrugs. Six feet of him went down that night in that damned old army jacket. He's had it on since high school; he's got it on now.
"Don't matter," he says. The grenade is back in his hand, pin in, and he's bouncing it up and down like an orange. "Sooner or later, it had to be something." He points up to the moon. "Remember me." Fucking Shakespeare, man. Hamlet.

Nineteen seventy five. I was born that year.

More pages are missing. I guess this guy went to Vietnam. My father did. But he's dead now, not from the war, but after. Overdosed on heroin. I hope it was an accident. My mother doesn't think so. Then she married this class A jerk, a probation officer.

Here's something.

15 January

And what happened after the rain? In the mud. Jeep stuck. First gear.

Tires spin. Throw it in reverse, spin. Winston, Santos, Gugliemino, their boots go suck, suck. Rain. Shoulders cushioned by spare tire mounted on the rear. Push. Gun that engine. Only thing worth gunning. I get out, too. Push and steer. Suck. Practically carry that jeep back to camp. Could have sworn I was in the shower. That's what the rain was like. Next day went out again. Same thing. Gives Sisyphus a new routine.

It could have been my father writing this. Rains like that up north all the time. He's right about the shower. It's like that itty bitty shower in the bathroom gets out of control, jumps out the window and takes over. I mean rain, rain, rain.

"Hey, babe, I'm home." It's Larry. Drunk, probably.
"Shut the door before the rain gets in."
"What the hell are you on?"
I laugh. "Thought I was back home for a second. Sounded like rain."
"Jesus Christ. Don't go hearing things on me."
Larry's hair is so yellow, I love it. Yellow with little flecks of white.
"You're early."
"Uncle Jack took up with some old babe at the bar." Larry makes a fist.
"Why? Sneaking somebody in here? Huh, doll?"
"Just this guy. Look. Here's a picture."

Larry picks up the diary, holds it up to the light bulb hanging down from the ceiling. A picture is glued on one of the pages. Four people stand in a row. On one end a man's face is circled. He's in a tux, not smiling. Underneath he's written "me." The face of the man next to him has a big X through it. In front of a small fountain, a woman in a white dress stands in the middle.

"Not too bad looking." Larry makes a fist again. "Now come to bed before I get jealous."
"No, I want to read more about this guy, he—"
Larry hits my cheek, hard.

I'm smart. I don't say anything. If my mother yells, my stepfather only goes after her harder. Larry nudges me in toward the bedroom.

The next day I'm watching the phones again at lunch time. I make the sofa bed up real nice and push it back into a couch. I watch a green car snake along the dirt road up to the office. It's the border patrol. Two cops. First time I've had to deal with them on my own. A tall, skinny guy gets out, walks in, his pointy boots shined up good. He kicks over the trash. "Get me Jack Slade. Official business."
"Not here."

He walks past me into the bathroom, steps back quickly. "Phew-ey!" He slams the bathroom door shut. "Where's his hired help?" He walks outside, back in. "Can't run a place this size without some help, huh Missy?"
I shrug.

I look behind him through the open door of the office. Not a Mexican in sight. One minute they're breaking down a semi, pounding like hell, then, silence. This has happened before. All three Mexicans, brothers, vanish into the shining air.

The cop jerks me right up off the sofa bed. Makes me go outside to look at his nasty dog in the back seat. Calls that dog "new equipment" to stop people from breaking the law.

I run back into the office, into the bathroom. I cry and cry. What if the juvey cops find me? The phone rings. I stay in the bathroom.

When Larry and his uncle get back, the cops are gone. Larry tells me not to worry. Border patrol comes around here every five minutes. His uncle says "No illegals work here, right honey? Just us three white folks, right honey? All-American white folks."

I go through a few cars in the afternoon, but I do it quick. I'm not in the mood. I find a five dollar bill folded up in an ashtray. I tuck it in my bra. I go back to the double wide. Larry's not there, but he's got Judge Wapner on. Thinks it'll keep me company.

I'm not in the mood for the Judge. I change the channel. What am I going to do? For right now, well, all I've got is the old vet.

I walk into the kitchen. The diary's not on the table. I walk around the trailer. Not many places for it to be. I go in the bedroom. Maybe Larry's been reading it. It don't see it. If it's not on the mattress, or on the floor, it's not anywhere. Back to the living room. Not on the TV. Not on the orange bean bag. I look in the refrigerator, take out a beer. I notice Larry's tied up the garbage. What's with him? He never ties up the garbage. I open up the bag. The diary's on top, the match stick still where I put it to mark my place.

11 March

Dark as shit out here. Too many trees in this Georgia swamp. Can't see the moon. Snake just dropped onto the car roof. Rage, rage, rage. Car light's gone. Just got me a bic lighter in operation. Rage against the dying of the light.
That's impolitic. Impolite. Impotent? What do I do, write a letter to my Congressman?
Dear Fucker—
Or to Columbus, the old bastard. Didn't discover anything besides his own ass. Columbus, c'est moi. Me.
P.S. Why bother? It's a black black hole no matter what. The black foot of a black ant on a black stone on a black night.

My father got in these moods. Black moods.

I turn back to the picture. A big tree with wide leaves and big flowers. "Magnolia," he's got written next to it. And under the picture he's got names of people. So faint. "Bus, Earl, Lily, C"—I can't make that out. Bus. That would be him. Is that a name?

I flip through, looking for more pictures. Nothing. The ink is too faded. Can't read most of it. Too bad. Must've got wet. Oh, here.

> 9 May

> *Her face. Moon of its own. Round, white. Eyelashes fan out in a half circle.*

Not much. A girlfriend?

I'm starved. Can't see me writing anything in a diary about Larry. I go over to the window. I watch the small fire shine out back. I go to sleep early.

Lunch time rolls around. Here's me heading back up to the office to look after the phones. What is it about this blue? Next to the white building it is even bluer than the rest of the sky. This, I would say, is impossible, except I have seen it with my own eyes. They say the Eskimos have all these words for snow. Probably, if they lived down here, they'd have a lot of words for blue.

It'll be a long lunch, Larry tells me. They've got to go out to Sierra Vista for some tires for his truck. Huge tires.

Just then one of the Mexicans shows up. He collects the pay for all of them on Fridays.
"Sorry, man." Larry's uncle takes three twenties from his billfold and places them on the counter. He turns his wallet upside down and shakes it. "Not good times."

The Mexican slowly picks up one twenty at a time, his small thumb carefully peeling them back. He looks at Larry's uncle. "Sixty is for one man each week."

Larry's uncle laughs. "What you going to do, sue me?"
The man shrugs.

Late afternoon, after they get back, I decide to head out for a different corner of the lot. I walk along the far edge of the property, marked by a couple strands of barbed wire. A purple butterfly swoops back and forth in front of me and settles on the wire. I see it isn't a butterfly, just one petal of a flower. I look around but I can't find where it came from.

In the back of a station wagon I see a tan suitcase with a thin red line running across it. I pull it out. A few faded stickers are half-peeled away. "Tucson" appears a few times. I push the latch but it doesn't give. I bang it on the ground. Nothing.

I see the key's in the ignition, but the battery's probably out. On a lark, I turn it over. The car doesn't start, but the radio goes on full blast. It's a Mexican station, with that singing polka music. It's cheerful and happy like the sky here.

I leave the radio on. I get my tools out. I still can't do anything with this suitcase. As I push it back into the rear of the station wagon, I happen to see green curtains slide across the window of an old rose-colored VW van two rows over.

I walk down that row on my way back to the office. At first glance, the VW looks like any of the other VW's scattered about the place. I notice that this one has wrap-around windows. Then I see a small skirt, a child's skirt, hanging off one of the side mirrors. No way. A kid in there?

I pass one of the Mexicans bouncing a pair of tires, fast, like balls in each hand. He smiles, nods. A red bandanna is wrapped around his neck. His face is wrinkled, but his body is small, light, like a cat.

By the time I get back to the office, it's closed. Another trek down to the trailer. Larry's not here. Shit.

I drag the diary out from under the mattress where I've hidden it. I sit there, flip through the pages. Nothing. Nothing more, that's it. Wait. Here on the back. It's the last thing.

> I wanted to go. I signed up even. Like they told you: get rid of the gooks, the Comm-u-nists. But one thing they didn't tell you. That face. A moon of its own. Is she still there? Alive? I brought her home with me, inside. Vietnam, too, inside.

I keep flipping through the pages. Nothing to do tonight. This is getting old fast. Real fast. One of the pages doesn't feel quite right, too thick. I get out my screwdriver. Carefully, I separate the pages.

> *12 June*
>
> Two men each sit on chairs in the kitchen. One is a vet, the other is, say, a Social Worker? No moon. It's in that land called Nosunandno-moonland.
> Vet: No light.
> Social Worker: It's night. (Gets up, flips light switch. Light does not go on).
> Vet: How many dead Vietnam vets does it take to change a light bulb?
> Social Worker: (Does not answer)
> Vet: 58,000. Ha, ha.
> S. W.: (Still does not speak)
> Vet: Get it? Dead? 58,000 men dead in veetnam. Change a light bulb? Change your thinking? Do you get it?
> S. W.: Oh, yeah (smiles). You mean you changed your mind?
> Vet: No shit, Sherlock.

Poor guy. A lot of regrets. My father could have written this. He changed his mind, too. My mother said he couldn't stand being called the gook sheriff.

I get a pen out of my tools. I write "How many runaways does it take to change a light bulb?" I can't think of anything. Then I write down

"One who got hit."

This damn diary is getting to me. I push the thing away.

I look out the kitchen window. There's that fire. I go out quickly, walk towards it.

I hang back outside the circle of light. The three brothers sit on old tires. One Mexican woman and a child sit there also. I haven't seen them before. The woman's black hair hangs loose down her back. A dark shawl is tied at her waist. She holds a small girl, her hair also long and loose, bright in the sheen of the fire. They look nice there, real nice. Nobody yelling at the girl. Just wait, I want to tell her. They'll be yelling soon enough. The woman turns plump husks of corn which have been laid in the fire. The men unfold the corn leaves and eat the tamales slowly, with their hands.

One of the men looks around. He talks to the others in a low voice. He looks in my direction again. He raises his hand, waves. In one motion, the woman gets up, picks up the child and walks down the wash toward the dark. The man scoops up the tamales from the fire with a blanket. He stops, takes a tamale and puts it on a stone. He waves again. Another man throws water on the fire from his canteen. Then they each walk away from me in a different direction.

I turn back, make the trip to the office, just in case Larry and his uncle are back. Nobody.

A car pulls up behind me. Border patrol. One of the cops from the other day. Not the mean one, the other one.

"Hey, Miss," he pulls his hand through his black hair. "I came to apologize." The car lights are on low beam, but they're aimed straight at me.
"Come here," he says.
Got a cigarette?" I walk over.

"Sure." He hands me one, leans back against the door. He lights it for me. "Hop in."

I kick at the front tire.

"You know, I got to thinking the other day." He lights up a cigarette, stares straight ahead. "My partner—he was out of line." He takes a drag. "I think you can help us." He takes another drag. "Hop in."
I don't move.
"You're a smart girl. I want to talk to you smart, okay?"
I nod. I walk around the passenger side. He pushes the door open. I slide in.

"You hear about the low pay around town?"
"Yeah." I look at his face, his hair. He's young, the youngest thing next to Larry I've seen around here. "You been doing this long?"
He shakes his head. "My first assignment."
But his hands, they're old. They're like old tree roots back home.
"Why's the pay low, you figure?"
"Nobody's got any money."
"Sure. And why's that? The wetbacks get in here and work for nothing." He reaches over towards the ashtray, stubs out his cigarette. "Illegal aliens." He extends an arm along the top of my seat; a circle of sweat under his arm stains his white shirt. "You know," he says softly. "I'm authorized to show our appreciation."

He takes out his wallet, fingers through it, pulls out a fifty dollar bill. He hands it to me. "You tell us about any Mexicans around the place, and the money's yours."
"I'll tell you what," I hand the bill back. "Let me get my purse. Then we can talk."
He taps a cigarette out of his pack, hands it to me. "Take your time. It's a nice evening. We'll talk."

I get out of the car, march down that quarter mile to the double wide. I figure I'll collect my things first. I can't stay here afterwards. A couple of stars shine out overhead. The blue's gotten deep now. Indigo. I'll take him to that rose-colored VW, the one with the clothes on the mirror.

I go in and get my large cloth purse. I stick some underwear in it, jeans and a T shirt. I tuck a beer inside. Oh yeah, the diary. I reach for it. No, I've got to travel light; I don't need that thing. I leave it on the table.

I walk down the steps of the double wide, happy. I'm going to get me some money today. Sayonara ol' Lare and Uncle.

It bothers me, that diary in there. I go back inside, get the diary and a pair of Larry's socks. I come down the steps again.

I look over at the old tires where the Mexicans were sitting. I walk over to where they set the fire. That tamale is still on the rock. I look back towards the border patrol car. I can't see it. I put the tamale in my purse. It's so quiet. I start walking again, but I just keep going in the same direction, heading toward the Interstate, which I can hear a long ways off to my left.

Emergence
Maria Leyba

You never knew my fathers
Who came from
Sacred ancient grounds
In Paquimé.
Traveled north
Merged with my
Apache Elders
Deep in the
Gila Wilderness,
Followed a daughter
To Barelas.

Oblivious to ancient ones
Sitting cross-legged
Outside my bedroom window
Smoking ceremonial pipes
Playing magical flutes
Chanting soothing songs.
Warm dark eyes
Never left me
Brilliant tunnels
That will someday
Guide me out of darkness.

You mocked my
Simple Indian ways
Claimed your Spanish sword
Wore a pretentious
Royal crown,

Tried to banish us
To frightful dungeons.

My children sat
With me, crushed
On the brick floor
In the adobe house
Without windows.
We clung to sweet juices
Of forbidden books
Slipped out of cocoons
Into infinity
Transitory freedom nipped
Our broken wings.

We awakened to
Icy vibrations rippling
Across brick floors
Your keys jingled
Against cold rusty bars
Gloomy frigid air
Snuffed out our lights
Black death slammed
The iron door,
Holding our breaths

We watched
Your menacing foul shadow
Loom over us,
Anger cut so deep
Into your ragged face
Filled with burning rage.

Terror seized
My children's eyes

Anxious beholders
Frozen
As they watched
Raw sewage spill
Out of your
Evil twisted mouth.

My tightened lips
Curled down
At one corner
Pointing south
Prayed as the children
Clawed the walls
Until the calm
Sacred nighttide
Sucked them out.

For weeks my Elders
Forewarned me
Of this maddening night
Of your demise,
I remained behind
Alone in my bedroom
As the ancient ones mandated
Together we chanted
Smoked pipes
Danced to rhythms
Of our people,
Courage enshrouded me
As I watched your
Diabolic volcano explode.

At sunrise
I EMERGED A WOMAN WARRIOR
Stood in my front yard

You sauntered past me
Your final last words
"Good Luck"
Ripped my mind,
I willed your pernicious
Evil spirit to fade
From my view forever.

At the crack of dawn
You called the police
So determined
To destroy us,
Six policemen entered
The sanctuary
Where my children
Slept peacefully.
Frigid metallic handcuffs
Pierced my heart
As they wrapped around
My 13 year old sons'
Slender wrists,
My primitive mournful cries
Exploded throughout Burque.

Tears blinded my
10 year old daughter
Rapid currents
Are tearing her
World apart,
Her tiny quivering body
Clings to me,
Ancient ones hold
Our trembling bodies
As we bury our

Shackles in the
Adobe without windows.

We endured five
Long lonely years
Obeyed the white man's law
Patiently waited
Tried to heal
Until my powerful son
Returned in the
Fall of his 18th year.

With his macho pride
He grips my shoulder
Dark intense eyes
Burning with conviction
Sear my memories
Husky voice plunges
Into my heart
Vows that no one
Will ever hurt
Or separate us
He will die to protect us
We are a
Familia Por Vida.

Proudly we walk
The streets of Barelas
Our voices blaring
Until we find
Your shriveled body
Fearfully running from us
Cowering in dark alleys
Petrified of
Seasoned warriors.

The Woman Who is Part Horse

Carla Jean Eardley

The woman who is part horse
Tends bar these days down at Diamond Dust.
Late on smoky nights
When old country and early Elvis
Limp from the jukebox in the corner
She pours red eye and beer on tap
Dances past the hungry hands.
These nights the men are hard and young
And thick-necked. They ought to
Be getting on down the road:
Got pregnant girls in rusty trailers
Waiting at the edge of town.
But they stop off at Diamond Dust
For a quick one with the grease
Still on their shirts
Just to see the pony woman. Of course
It doesn't show to strangers:
Just cheekbones and hair like molasses
In the summer sun and that way her hips
Move when she slides between the tables.
But when they offer sweaty nights
In the shadows of the big rigs
Her eyes are horse eyes and they back off.
She grins and wipes the glasses they abandon.
Two o'clock means end of shift
Cold stars and the hard road up the hill
Just waiting for hooves.
When she locks up those doors
She'll gallop
To the moon.

Cooking Beans

Glenda Stewart Langley

I sit here cooking beans
While the poet I'm reading writes from
        a nest of drug-crazed punks in the Village
to glowing reviews.

"Don't forget to set the lid ajar,"
        my husband reminds me.
"Or they won't cook down."

"You always forget."

I get a letter from Cynthia
She's starting a new job—executive vice president
            in Paris.

Damn—these beans need more garlic
        and I'm out.

Yesterday at lunch with Teresa
She's just back from Mexico City
        —she saw de Meq conduct—he was magnificent

"Don't these beans need more salt?"

Yes, but then they'll make your feet swell.

Deborah calls—they've just got a multi-millionaire
couple to sponsor their theater company
        every performance   a sell out

"Don't forget to stir them—you burned
the ones on the bottom last time, remember?"

> Because of the job, Cindy says, they'll be living apart...
> Terry asks me whether she'll ever meet the right someone...
> Deb says he's moved out of her bedroom, what should she do...

"Babe—they're done! They're great! You refry 'em—
> I'll roll the tortillas—we'll make it to payday yet!"

And his smile like the sun through the clouds reminds me
Nobody loses all the time.

Moving Towards Morning

Jacqueline D. Moody

I.

Looking out the classroom
window at the
trees.
She wants to be a tree.
She reaches up and leaves
sprout from her
fingertips.

She keeps busy.
By day
her heels echo
in every
hallway. At night
she wraps herself in
words, like pulling a
sweater around her shoulders.

This woman breathes eloquently.

Shh, listen, you can
hear it.
For years now there's been this
hole widening in her
heart. She speaks
loud to drown
it out—the sound of her own
heartbeat getting hollow

like a sob in a
cathedral.

II.

When I was younger and my
hips moved to a song in my head,
I wanted to ask her
are you in love?
have you ever danced alone in
your house, the music
loud and the lights out? and
do you ever write poetry in
your head, doing sixty across
loop 1604 at dawn?

When I was younger
and cancer stole
my brother and then my
innocence

she was there.

Perhaps cancer *is*
contagious, somehow—or
maybe it's a side
effect of heartbreak.
Or maybe god *is* a
man.

It's taking her, too. It's
gonna eventually

piss out that
fierce
beautiful carnivorous
dark light
in her eyes.

And I don't know who to pray
to anymore but I pray
anyway: La Virgen,
Venus, Isis
whoever—
Let me please be half
the woman she is.

III.

Her soul is seamless now.

She carried the weight of
the world
gladly, and without it
she moves
diurnally
above horizons,
riding Cassiopeia's
throne, reining
stars
behind her.

I wrap my sweater around my shoulders.

Her grave
is bone solid

limestone. Kneeling
here, the hematite
soil stains my
jeans and my hands
red.
I rub my eyes
and my tears are
red.

This close
to the ground I can
feel the earth
turning, I can
hear the gears
grinding.
First I crawl,
then I run,
pushing
the continents underfoot,
tripping in latitudes,
following
the stars from one
sunrise to the
next.

We keep the earth
spinning, she and I.

Los Tucsonenses

Jessica Jaramillo

A truck load of brown-skinned
men diligently go to work.

A group of sun-kissed children
obey the cross guard as they
go to their bilingual elementary
school.

Father Trevizo holds a Spanish
mass for three hundred parishioners.

Ten well-dressed Cholos walk into
Escandalo's Night Club.

Rosa and her family of eleven
wait to be served at Mi Nidito's.

A Tata for the sixteenth time,
Don José receives a congratulatory
hand-shake.

"Los Diablos" kick their soccer ball
straight past the goalie.

A group of "MECHA" students march
their way through campus demanding
more funding.

The Mexican American Veteran's Association
prepares their float for this year's parade.

Doña Eusebia's sewing club meets at
ten am sharp to make pillow cases.

Chicanos Por La Causa dedicates another
home to a low-income family.

Carolina reads her "Spanglish" poem
to "Mujeres Que Escriben."

Patchwork Life

Sharon Creeden

My life is a quilt,
Hand sewn from bits and pieces.
Random patterns, textures, colors.
Original and incomplete.

Patches made from
My satin wedding dress,
Mexican-loomed cotton from my storyteller's vest,
Wool from my lawyer's suit.

Stitched together with remnants of
Denim worn by a teen-aged day dreamer,
Flowered flannel baby blankets,
Ribbons from braids.

Some people suggested,
"Follow a traditional design."
"Use more pieces of the same fabric."
"Enroll in a quilting class."

There never was a pattern
I cared to use all the way.
I made it up
As I sewed.

Not a gift;
Not a museum hanging;
Not for sale at the county fair.
Made to keep me warm.

Russian Wedding

Maria-Elena Wakamatsu

Que lejos estoy del suelo en que nacido...
(Canción Mixteca)

I HAVE NEVER been married. Here I am 41 years old and I have never been married. A disgrace to my family, my people, those who think a decent Mexicana should be married when she's the prettiest, or at least as pretty as she's going to get, right around 18. I suppose I never quite got as pretty as I was going to get, not at 18 anyway. At 18, I was really dark. "Prieta" me decían, "India" when they thought they were offending me, and "Negra" when I'd really pushed it playing in the sun all day long and my mother thought she would insult me into taking better care not to get so dark. "¿Ya basta, no? Te estás poniendo como teléfono." But to get married you have to feel that the loyalty you feel is reciprocated, qué no? That the one you hug, hugs you back, qué no?

I never developed that kind of connection to this country either. No one seemed terribly eager to welcome me here. Nah, Mrs. Swengel, my first grade teacher in rural Yuma County didn't even speak a word of Spanish and I, well, yo no hablaba ni papa de inglés. The day I couldn't hold it in anymore and I started squirming in my seat, that day when she made absolutely no effort to recognize International Bathroom Language and she forced me to say *something* to her, something that felt like rocks in my mouth and sounded like "Pro-feh-soh-rah, may day-ha eer all bah-nyo?" that day I felt the meanness of a country whose cruelty to children is unsurpassed. That day, I felt abandoned and I realized I was unwelcome in my land.

It was a glorious autumn morning in Moscow. The city was teeming with the hustle and bustle of a busy people boarding and deboarding clean, electric buses where people pay their fare on the honor system. The bus driver never even makes sure that you paid your fare. Men and women step quickly and with determination up and down the sidewalks lining the vast boulevards six and eight lanes wide. I was struck by the orderliness of their activity, the politeness of these people. For as busy as they were, they seemed to be happy with their lives.

The bus stopped at Red Square and all twenty of us got out. We were to be there for three months. Talk about explosive. Get twenty organizers in one room for any reason and see what happens. Beneath the surface of vision and selflessness, lurks a monstrous ego and arrogance, and compañeros who are far better at exploiting women than any imperialist ever could be. Anyway, they'd all brought their cameras and were now fumbling around with the cases, loading the film, and just so eager to start shooting. Me, I brought my eyes and ears wide-open. I find it disrespectful to record images of sacred things. La Catedral de San Basilio was a strange sight. The huge onion-like domes sitting on top of those towers gave it an almost comic effect. Don't get me wrong, it was magnificent, gargantuan, and its very unique appearance made me shudder with the energy of a deeply religious people...and I felt their strength.

In front of Lenin's Tomb, the changing of the guard was starting. "Apúrate, te lo vas a perder," me gritaba Petra. The mechanical precision turns. The long extension through the legs. The lonely echo of shiny, black boots against concrete. The dark gray military uniforms lined in red. The hats poised on the proud brows of gorgeous young men. The solemnity heavy in the air. The silence thick and pregnant with the pride of a forsaken people...and I felt their reverence.

The Tomb of the Unknown Soldier was our last stop before lunch and the line was longer than any I've ever seen at Disneyland. Petra had been here many times and besides, she was meeting Alexei for lunch.

"Vámonos, ¿sí? Luego venimos." She and I could do that, just take off without the rest of the group because, well, Alexei and Dolores could bring us later. Alexei was the head of the Federation of Soviet Labor Unions and Dolores was his counterpart in Mexico. But I didn't want to go just then. Somehow, this was more important than any man could ever be. "¿Sabes qué? Vete tú. Yo te alcanzo al rato."

The line was moving slowly and I deliberately fell behind the rest of the group. I wanted to be surrounded by these people. I was witnessing the most sacred connection they have with one another. The love and respect they have for their country bonds a people, a whole nation with an irrevocable unity of purpose against even the most formidable of foes. How absolutely delicious, intoxicating...and I felt delirious.

"¿Mexicanski?" me preguntó una mujer.
"Da," my Russian was very limited, pero mis deseos de conocerla, de saber por qué había tanta gente, por qué visitan esta tumba, todo esto me salía por los ojos, por los poros.

"Ah, que bien." Y llenándose de orgullo, de satisfacción, "Bienvenida. ¿Como le gusta nuestro país?" "Me encanta." Lo decía de todo corazón.

"¿Cómo es que sabe Ud. hablar español?" "Oh, nosotros le tenemos mucho cariño a Mexico." Her voice was like melcocha.

Era cierto. En el camión, en el metro, en la calle, la gente me paraba, me saludaba. Hablan inglés y español, todos. Aquella gente en ese país tan desconocido, tan prohibido. Aquella gente tan fraternal, tan educada, tan limpia—ni un chicle, ni una basurita tirada en la calle. Aquella gente sabe más de México que yo.

"Explíqueme algo por favor, ¿sí?"

"Por supuesto," me contestó con una paciencia y dulzura que nunca tuvo la Mrs. Swengel. Me intrigaban las parejas de recién casados. Allá en frente se veian dos novias vestidas sencillas, de blanco y de velo. Los maridos sonrientes y ellas radiantes. "¿Qué hacen esos novios aquí?" La catedral estaba cerrada y el registro civil, pues, aquí no erá.

"Mire, señorita," me dijó, su voz llenándose de tristeza, "en nuestro país, no tuvimos la protección de una Virgen, ni de un Dios que se acordará de nosotros. Cristo no pasó por aquí. Nadie, señorita, nos dio la mano. Durante la guerra, perdimos la mitad de la población y toda la industría. Nos quedamos sin casa, sin pan, sin una mano que nos ayudará. Ahora, despues de 70 años de batallar solos en este mundo, a los que les damos las gracias son a ellos, a los soldados que por nosotros dieron la vida. A ellos y a esta Madre Patria le dan las gracias y piden la bendición.

Weddings in the Soviet Union made me cry. The loyalty they pledge to one another is deeply and inexorably pledged to their country, and for that...they must love and understand themselves and one another very well. No wonder I stood there and wept...no wonder I've never been married...

Light at Dusk

Evamaria Lugo

I WALK into the main room at the end of the day and there is no one there. I always feel safe and welcomed in our home. Daylight is tiptoeing her way out as I patiently wait for the other lady of the house. I smile a grateful smile while facing the window next to the garden. It is good that no one is here yet. I need to clear the dark cloud in my heart. I can center my thoughts in this silence. I can think of beauty, of peace. I can think of my lover's face and quiet ways.

Was it luck that we found each other two years ago? Somehow, the minute I saw her, I knew that we were meant to be together. That day, the unsuspecting hermit I was walked towards the opposite end of the room and made polite conversation to friends while observing her. It was a self-imposed challenge not to go near her. I feared that something in me would rush over and protect her with an embrace.

Or was I the one that wanted to feel protected? Maybe I hoped that after all the years of sadness and loneliness, the gods were ready to reward me and offer joy?

Joy...it really is an appropriate name for her. I wish her mother was alive so I could ask her about my lover's childhood. Did Joy fill life with beauty even then? Did her gentle daughter love strawberries even then? I should ask Joy if she had always loved strawberries; but more importantly, I should ask her if it is true that she is having an affair with someone else while being my lover, my partner, the love of my life, the person I want to see smile at me more than I want anything else in the world.

I remember her first smile... it made me blink, it was so loving. I held her extended hand and acted politely indifferent when a friend brought her over to my corner and introduced her to us. I wanted to do something insane and romantic like get down on one knee before her and kiss her hand. I wanted to offer her my life in return for another smile and when I heard her voice I knew that I would be hers.

I took my time being honest about my feelings of love for her. In our circle it is tempting to believe that someone cares for you just because they buy you lunch. Maybe we are too needy as a people. Maybe all the ingrained independence is just a cover-up for unspeakable need. I have never even told her I love her. Why allow yourself to be so vulnerable? There are no guarantees, you know.

I will act suave when I see her tonight and just say something like: Darling, I met Peter outside my studio just now and he told me that he had seen you being very friendly to Ellen at a restaurant today.

Should I worry? Should I call Ellen to a duel? Should I be stoic, like my ancestors and suffer in silence? I think that homosexuals have an innate tendency to be insecure about intimate relationships. Society, after all, does not even acknowledge our existence. Why should our emotional commitments have any value?

And yet when I think of my lover I think about our mutual satisfaction at showing love. She buys my favorite coffee for breakfast. I buy her favorite teas for dinner. I make sure that no one disturbs her when she is practicing her music, and she protects my private time when I am writing. We have learned our special wants and needs...we know how to forgive each other our frailties. She has taught me to love...I really see and understand light and color when she is around. I have never met anyone on whom light looks as lovely. I have never met anyone who can call out my name like she does. I should be strong. So what if she also leaves...one more thing to try to forget from my list of broken relationships. One more reason to be antisocial again...the last reason?

But wait. I am not giving her up this easily. I am a worthwhile human being capable of love. I know that I make her happy. I know that I am worthy of her. I know...

She walks into the room and slowly starts turning the lights on.

"Good, you are here. We should buy timers for these lamps. You look pensive and almost sad next to the window, dear."
"Oh, pensive? Yes, I actually am."

Light and her presence changed the room that had slowly turned dark. I have also changed.
"Is everything all right, sweetie?"

"Yes, now that you are here, all is well. I was just remembering when we met. I was thinking how fortunate I feel. Tell me about you, Joy, how was your day?"

"Boring. Except for lunch, I asked Ellen out so she would give me a ride to the new bookstore you and I discovered last week. I wanted to give you the poetry book you liked. I promise you, someday we will have lots of money and fame and I will be able to buy you expensive gifts, castles in Spain, villas in Italy, bookstores everywhere, a couple of museums, and the moon too... In the meantime, happy anniversary."

"Thank you, this is lovely." One of my hands holds the book and the other touches her face.
"I am glad you like it."

The hermit is ready to grow up after all. Yes, I am still afraid. The possibility of a heartbreak will always be there. My life is on the line here but surely people have felt this before and have dared to follow their hearts. I am not the first person in the world who has known raw fear and survived.

"I have a gift for you also." My heart is pounding and my hand trembles as I slowly draw her close to me and kiss her lips, after I murmur softly and shyly: "I have never said this to you before...I love you."

"You always know how to wrap a gift," she says, smiling.

Grace

Carmela Delia Lanza

"She is the smell of good mud..."
Clarissa Pinkola Estés, Ph.D.
<u>Women Who Run With the Wolves</u>

A hunchbacked woman carries a pail of water to her house
and a naked child walks toward the donkey
kicking a dust cloud into the eyes of the man
across from me coughing and looking at his watch.
I have been smelling my grandmother on my body these days
as I try to sleep, to eat,
I taste her walking down the hall,
the sound of her bedroom door
and I understand now
all that she was, without speaking a word.

In my darkened room,
the eyes tell stories instead of dreams,
singing instead of words and I am smoothing myself down
using tears and a waxing moon as my tools,
changing the story again,
and I will reflect hard enough and find
the deserted, empty public pool by the highway as
we drove by it every Sunday
on the way to my grandmother's house,
what happened to the people, the water?
I have seen that pool again
after twenty years,
and I feel the weight of the china closet key in my hand
and she is winking, telling me to go on

and take another cookie,
go on, she whispers in Italian and the kitchen light burns
a hole through the center of my body.
And I dig deeper into the soil,
what is my grave, what is my food.

I will leave now and birth my own familiar house,
where the bones and skin are all my own smells, my own tongue,
where the turtle in the backyard
carries the heat of the day on her back
without using language,
and I never say a word to the tree of thorns,
I only bow and respect, and bury gifts of this world
out of fear and desire.

I will hold one foot in the ocean and the other on the mesa,
and I do not miss the ocean because
I am living in a prehistoric sea;
there are only ghosts of shells embedded in rock
and I am hardening into a fossil day by night,
finding ghosts of myself in the laundry room or the cellar.
You will not find me groping for the perfect word anymore,
the easy joke, the pleasure house of existing, of having fun—
it all fossilized during the last Great Drought;
I am finally the Mother of the Dead calling out to you,
reminding you of your own ultimate test,
I do not seek for what I have already lost,
I have lost most of my tongue,
I have lost some of my children,
I cannot remember my dreams.
I will not answer the phone because
desire disappeared along with my last laugh
and last warning in the muck.
Falling in love is a ritual I vaguely remember

my mother teaching me,
along with the command, "Don't lose your lunch money."

I walk by a man stretched on the street,
blood under his head,
and I whisper my blessing, "Grace."
I am the mother dolphin swimming past the coffin-builders
who mold aluminum, wood, velvet coffins all day and then
go home to a warm supper,
and there is all the land I want in this undiscovered country.
I am not a prisoner of your boundaries anymore,
waking in my dream, breathing,
holding the worms between my fingers in prayer.

Deglazing the Pan

Sharon DiMaria

The hardest bones to clean lie small
at the base of the back where wings connect
and bits of bread collect cupped in vertebrae,
congealed with memory and laden with fat.

Years before, our foremothers
might have removed the keel and
scraped some carcass clean enough for wearing,
or honed ulna and radius to spear fish,
or laced string through the hollow centers
and worn them simple.

Now it is better not to display
the skeletal remains,
but to boil them discreetly for broth,
conceal them hidden and frozen
on less frequented shelves.

Unpacking the bird extracts volumes of
holiday treyf, past celebrations, faint
recollections steam nebulously
like a new kill on the road.

Uncles who arrive widowed and conspicuously early,
bearing the unfashionable names of the very old,
railroad watch in pocket, abundant with time,
eyebrows bushed and disheveled, wild like sage.
There is too, the clothing of old uncles.
Suspect in suspenders,

trousers balloon obsolete in their pleats,
cuffed for some old war.
And the tables laid larger, more opulent in memory,
the dead less vexatious, the young less unruly.
The rivalries not so bitter.

We remember ourselves brilliant with childhood,
coiled with expectation
bursting to transcend the truss of celebration
and run along the twisted banks of ditch
and field
until our clothing is burred
and we stink with a soup of sweat and dust
and our own trouser legs
stiffen black with bicycle grease.
And we are unrepentant.

Somehow childhood endures us
and we become taut with conceit,
a holiday nebula.
We parade ourselves saints in hollow procession,
vestments pinned with small miracles
and guilty donations to the dead.
More perfect and endless
we flash back from our past
absorbent
and threatening.

Others arrive impassive
sag and crease weightless in age
to hang like aphids
on the underside of each minute.
Self-smitten, bewitched by ourselves
we cannot texture their mystery.
They will live with us in a hundred houses

stare back from kitchen windows
unfeatured and minimal
their faces disjointed narratives
a lined history to crave
a why.

Somewhere memories
merge into each other
undulate like lovers.
Blind in deceit
they conspire to make us
appear better,
less guilty.

Today I pour hot liquids, warm riesling
to loosen the scrapings,
the clotted juices
from the bottom of the pan.
This rendering occurs yearly.

Outside from Pastura, down to Tomé,
and even south to Vegita,
the snow geese, the heron, the sage grouse and others
pluck the marsh fields
of corn and seeds, stand knee high in water
their legs bent stalks, thin as wheat.
Abruptly they fly in formation,
honk overhead to the
unfortunate cousin I dismember below.
They call back in time to Archaeopteryx* lying
distinct, thwarted forever in Mesozoic limestone.
Imbedded.
Frozen.
Abundant with time.

Archaeopteryx or "ancient wing" was unearthed in Bavaria in 1861 and is the oldest bird fossil so far discovered.

Way Back on Solano Street

Jill A. Oglesby

Dawn

I WAS BORN in old St. Joseph's hospital in downtown Albuquerque, New Mexico, on the third floor on a cold morning in February. You know old St. Joseph's—it's that red brick building, about three stories high, that you can see from Interstate 25 with the big, modern high rise behind it that they call new St. Joseph's.

The week I was born, my father's mother, Mamaw, had been out visiting from Texas, and she'd taken my mother on a ride in the station wagon out on the mesa down a bumpy dirt road. She told my mother it was an old wives' tale that that would make the baby come, although they used to do it in a wagon. Around midnight of the same day, my mother went into labor.

It was 1965, the age of science. No, I mean the *Age of Science* with capitals. Mother was whisked away in a sterilized wheelchair, and my father was told to scram—no fathers allowed.

The doctors worked over my mother, saying "Ah ha," and "Oh, oh," pretending amongst themselves that they had invented birth and this woman out back in the laboratory. They gave my mother a "saddle block" anesthetic as if she were a horse. They said, "Come here, baby, come here, baby," coaxing me out.

I was born without blood and without afterbirth pre-wrapped in a pink-for-girls sanitized blanket at three in the morning and placed in an incubator among the other sanitized babies.

Later, when my mother had had the opportunity to repair her hair and makeup, and my father had composed himself, the nurses brought me in to see my parents in my mother's semi-private room. My mother held me to her bosom, smiled deep into my eyes, put a bottle to my lips, and said, "Be an engineer. It's a good career field for women."

My father, overcome with emotion, said, "Dallas Cowboys. Your country. First and ten. Home run." A group of nurses, behind him, cheered, shook their pom poms, and performed a random number of back flips and split jumps with beaming enthusiasm.

And seven angels flew out the hospital window in seven different directions proclaiming the news.

Deep in the Navajo Nation, an elder looked up briefly and said in passing, "That's not true there was no afterbirth."

At a pueblo on the Rio Grande, a little girl only one and one-half years old said, "The nuclear family is not the be-all and end-all of experience."

In Waxahachie, Texas, Comoma, my mother's mom, said, "Life is one fool thing after another. Love is two fool things after each other." She was just reading the plaque on her kitchen wall, wondering why she'd woken up so early for no good reason. Usually, she slept until 5:00 in the morning.

And at home, in the brown stucco house on Solano Street, my big brother, who was 1.5 years old himself, waddled up to Mamaw holding his blanket and sucking his thumb and said, "Hopital babee Mommy dying?" and started to cry. Mamaw reached out her big catfish hands and pulled him into her lap and said, "Hush now, you. You'll be just fine," and tried not to promise anything she couldn't deliver.

Just After Dawn

My parents brought me home in the station wagon on an old dirt road they now call Spain. I had black, black baby hair until my hair fell out and grew back in brown.

It was 1965, as I mentioned before, and we didn't know that the nuclear family wasn't the be-all and end-all of experience. That's how we lived, one nuclear family out in the Great American West, with capitals. To my parents, the little house on Solano Street was a sod house on the prairie or a ranch house or Ft. Oglesby.

Of course, there was the extended family—my mother's brothers, my father's sister, the cousins spilling out all over when they came to visit, the grandparents, the great grandparents and great aunts and great uncles. They were just over there in Texas, which was another country next door to New Mexico and 12 hours away by car.

On Solano Street, we had the YWCA, the neighborhood, the Methodist church we belonged to, the trips out in the country to see old wagon roads and Indian ruins, the trips to the old Spanish colonial town called Old Town, the trips to the pueblos, arts and crafts, bottles of cold soda pop in every color, eat your spinach, cottage cheese because Mom was on a diet, our dogs Paco and Jacques, the street sweeper, my brother getting beat up, and Dad's secret job at Sandia National Labs, where they even locked up the typewriter ribbons at night so the Russians wouldn't get them.

We had marriage and family comes before your friends and ambitions and the church comes before everything else. We had trips to the mountains in the snow. We had you are from Scotland and Ireland and England, and I wish I was an Indian kid, Mom. I wish I had black hair, Mom.

We always had enough to eat, and Mom had too much because she always wanted to lose weight.

We had New Mexico all around us, and the United States was out there somewhere in the distance, perhaps located in the television. Except that's who my father worked for.

It was 1965, and we thought we were one nuclear family making all our own decisions, Mom, Dad, Sis, and Brother, out on the Western frontier, the Great American West, where the liberal part of the 1960's passed my parents right by like a dust storm in the distance (I think we were in church at the time).

Morning

The truth is, I think all the time about my afterbirth. People say the place your afterbirth is buried is the land you are tied to. So what did old St. Joseph's hospital do with the afterbirth of babies and other "medical wastes" in 1965? I've thought of going over there and asking them. Was it incinerated? Did it go to the city dump? I've even thought of locating the city dump they were using in 1965 and standing on the edge to see if I feel a tug at my belly button.

Maybe it's Solano Street I'm most tied to, or Albuquerque, or New Mexico. Maybe it's the Methodist church. Maybe it's just my nuclear family, Mom, Dad, Brother, and Sis. Maybe it's my extended family.

Way back when we lived on Solano Street, we had an ornamental peach tree that flowered in the spring, two Italian cypresses standing guard over the entrance to the garage—one on either side—long-needled pine trees, grass, and a rose bush island on the far side of the driveway. Out back, we had a huge oak tree, lots of grass, a swing set, clotheslines, and a concrete slab. Out beyond the grass, which sloped downward, was the wall. The wall had little dents in it with gates for setting out the garbage. Beyond the wall was the mesa, which was scrubby and bare, with big city streets off in the distance giving off hot automotive smells.

The front door faced east, towards the Sandia mountains. The back door faced west, towards Mt. Taylor.

Nearby, there was a store that had a 20-foot concrete arrow in the parking lot. It said: Here is your childhood; Your childhood is here.

We always had enough to eat. We always had enough.

Some Familiar Artifacts of the Southwest

Lorraine Ray

ELEGANT KLEPTOMANIACS winter in the Southwest of the past. They open the rear door of the family car with a sunny smile and steal a boy's navy blue sailor coat fresh from the cleaners. By April they've left the desert for San Francisco.

Starlets, whose husbands have been recently killed in bizarre ballooning accidents in the Punjab, flee the Hollywood press and mourn anonymously in the dark adobes of our old pueblos. The local dude ranch hosts an English princess who aspires to ride western-style, while a fabulously wealthy Eastern woman (an heiress of a vast cold cream fortune) briefly owns the corner desert lot, the one with the dead dog and the trashed '49 Chevy. Crossing that same vacant lot on her way to kindergarten, a girl brushes her winter coat against a stand of cholla, detaching a joint of the cactus onto the hem of her coat. Feeling the spines stab her, she runs blindly ahead and disappears into the school screaming the alarming testimony, "Jumping cactus got me!" When the Women's Botanical Club holds their annual meeting near another cholla patch, an old lady visiting the Southwest from Toledo promptly topples backwards in her Mexican leather chair. She is brought upright again and offered a tiny cup of Ibarra chocolate.

During rodeo week, ladies with bouffant hairdos don slender, peg-legged Levi's that zip up the back or the side. There is a school rodeo square dance. Grimacing horribly throughout, little girls touch the flushed, fleshy palm of unpopular boys. No one understands the caller on the warped phonograph record.

One Saturday noon as the air raid sirens wail, the silly man on the television animal show unlocks a portable cage and gets bit by a molting coyote named Bob. The next Monday at school everybody's giggling about that coyote.

It's the duty of every child to cross the border into Mexico and thereby save the taxes on a fifth of rum. Childless couples corral the neighborhood children into the back of their station wagons to fulfill this mission. The children beg to be bought paraffin skulls full of colored sugar water, clicking Mexican jumping beans infested by the larva of a minuscule moth, and rag dolls without legs (but with a second head under their skirts).

Mothers warn that Valley Fever's in the mud, nevertheless, hearing river toads singing in the arroyos each summer, the children vanish, clutching empty peanut butter jars, into the realm of the Harry Man and the tadpole.

A withered old bitter-looking woman turns her Pontiac with its Indian-head hood ornament straight toward a huge pink dust devil. Perceiving it directly in front of her, she comes out of her angry thoughts into a furious race to crank up her window before being sand blasted.

A young woman in the modern dance troupe drops out of high school and becomes a stripper at the Blast-Off Bar near the Air Force base. The sons of Apache Indian fire fighters mutely attend art classes, then join the marines. The Ox-bow Saloon continues to serve the coldest beer.

Cousins in the East remark that a real Christmas doesn't exist in the Southwest; Santa Claus piñatas with their curly white tissue paper beards grin in response. The evenings before Christmas are spent building puzzles (incongruously, of English thatched cottages and looming Bavarian castles), uncovering plump raisins in the bellies of tamales, and laughing at the zany man on television whose couches are all "gangas."

From the screened windows of a crumbling desert tubercular sanitarium, the wind carries the sound of hideous, hacking coughs. People with slack mouths can be seen staring at a sea of weird, waving creosote, a graveyard where they plan to be buried.

Snake skins puff up and whisk away in golden hoops across lawns of gravel colored pink, and green, and turquoise. A girl rakes the colored gravel in swirling patterns and watches a molting coyote wittily navigate main street.

Vegetables

Alicia Z. Galván

I PEEL the cucumber, careful not to remove more cucumber than skin. Then I rummage for another one, searching among the mound of vegetables that will be transformed into tonight's dinner. I pick out the next one, frowning and tossing it aside because it is too bruised. Not rotten. Just too soft and uneven.

Visual images slip out from my memory where they are held, restrained in a distant past, believed to be no longer practical in the present.

~ ~ ~

The truck would come around and stop by twice a week. It was an older model vehicle, with dented rusty metal bumpers and rubber tires patched repeatedly. Increasing age made it sputter as it made its way into the open alley. The rear compartment often overflowed with vegetables. A cornucopia of edible possibilities!

The craggy old gentleman wore an old sweat-stained hat, a threadbare long-sleeved cotton shirt and khaki pants, always worn low on his stomach. He was missing some front teeth and this made him sputter as he spoke, just like the truck he owned. He was a street produce vendor with several regular customers on his route.

He would drive downtown in the early hours of the morning to the big market place, hunting down the choicest and freshest produce he could find. When his search was finished, he would temptingly arrange fruits and vegetables like colorful jewels in small straw baskets. His clientele counted on him for freshness, and were willing to pay a little more for this personal service. He would sell them only the best, picking out the produce painstakingly as they looked on.

At the end of his day twice a week, he would pass by our house. He was a welcome sight when he made his customary appearance. He would call out, telling us to come out of our two room wooden shack that I knew as home. No words of persuasion were needed. Then he would hand out the small straw woven baskets piled high with vegetables.

Tomatoes, discarded because they were not red enough, or too red and mushy. Onions with black mold creeping up beneath the thin skins. My mother said the tomatoes and onions were just right for making huevos rancheros. She coaxed the old man into giving her a few serrano chiles to make the cooked chile salsa. If he was hungry, he would even go buy the eggs as well. There we were, enjoying breakfast in the middle of the afternoon or late in the evening. It was truly a feast, because we didn't get to eat eggs very often. There was no money to buy them.

Some of the oranges and lemons had dried spots on them, meaning they could be just as dry inside or spots of green mold on them, which meant they were past their prime. I did not care. It was worth the gamble to discover a sweet juicy one.

Odd sized and shaped squash, tossed aside because a small triangular core sample had revealed too many seeds, became a thin vegetable soup mixed along with some still respectable looking ears of corn that we cut up into small pieces. There was no meat in this soup—money was scarce for us.

Some bananas, when we received them, were fighting a losing battle with fruit flies on their stems and skins. Some were much too ripe, but if you searched well and hard there were still some firm areas that were salvageable.

Pears and apples too small or not bright enough to entice his best customers were warmly greeted at our house. If they were not sweet enough, we sprinkled some grains of salt over them, providing a tart contrast for the taste buds. Salt was the only condiment we had in abundance, and it was used to season almost everything, like sprinkling it on a watermelon because it was not very sweet.

And then, of course, there were the cucumbers. Some had bruised spots, but were aromatic and tasty nonetheless. A special ritual was involved with eating a cucumber. Before you ate it, you had to slice off the stem end and rub both parts of the cucumber together. Often a white gummy residue would form, and the ritual performed was believed necessary to reduce gastric bloating upon consumption. I took great delight in the adventure of preparing the cucumber, carving out and slicing the firmer chunks into rounds, then sprinkling them with the juice coaxed out from an almost dry lemon.

~ ~ ~

In my childhood innocence, I processed all these events as ordinary occurrences that happened to everyone. My eagerness and optimism did not and could not grasp the severity of the times. I don't remember being bitter because we were poor.

Now I know we were among those that are labeled indigent and poverty-stricken. The old man would unload his undesirable vegetables with us out of pity. He never charged us a penny. We were his charity case twice a week. As bruised, mushy and overripe as the fruits and the produce were, I only tasted the sweet nectar of nourishment they promised.

We must have presented a desperate and sorry sight for him to stop by and visit with us, giving us what he might otherwise throw away. Nevertheless, it was his intention that mattered. Looking back, I hope that that even he benefited from the warmth of human contact that comes from sharing.

~ ~ ~

A high-pitched child's voice pleading with me and small hands tugging at me return me to the present.

"I am hungry. When will supper be ready?"

I re-examine the cucumber that I have just rejected and tossed aside. It's not really all that bad. True—it would never win a prize for most beautiful vegetable in its color and appearance, but it is edible. At least there are no molds or mushy areas. Peeling it, I smile and perform the old but familiar ritual saved from my childhood. I eat a piece and find its taste as unique as the memories it has unleashed, glad I gave it a second chance.

I laugh quietly and my daughter insists on knowing why. I catch myself about to say "Nothing," and stop. Instead, I get a chair and stand her on it.

"I am going to show you how to cut and eat a cucumber," I say to her. We spend the next ten minutes playing and giggling as I now teach her how to cut and enjoy a cucumber. Love and memories are shared and a humble tradition born in poverty seems destined to go on. Life is good.

Ondas on Her Tongue

Dolissa Medina

I AWOKE with the ocean in my bed. That was how she came to me. Salty, she swam toward flesh, planting her naked torso on my thigh. Fishtail tightened around my muscle; her cancion seeped into my blood. As the voice filled my veins I felt her grito through my spine. This is how she came to me. She has not left me since.

It has been several years since that moment when I first woke up with a Sirena lover in my bed. But like the instinctual, unnamed desire of the young queer, my adult introduction to the woman of the sea was merely a matter of reunion. In this liquid visitation, a long-forgotten girlhood intrigue was reborn within me, and with it, a return to a cultural past. That place: the warm, quiet nights of South Texas, where young children still hear the wails of La Llorona. Only when I was a girl, I never listened to her cries. I was too busy singing with mermaids.

"La Sirena"—I remember her arms reaching out toward my grandmother's hands as they placed the card with the small image before me. My childish eyes would search for a match on the game board. With a fistful of raw beans in my tiny hands, I would find the sea creature's mate—another naked Sirena, wading and waiting there between pictures of the sun and the moon. I'd place a single bean on the game board and my grandmother would again touch the deck, drawing another image.

I often played this card game while sitting on top of my abuelita's bed; her sabanas registered in my memory as a faded but deep, intense blue. From those first moments of visual connection, I was becoming aware of the ritualistic power of symbol: of all 54 images I repeatedly saw in the Lotería card deck, only La Sirena lingered with an intensity unparalleled until much later in life. There was something odd yet fascinating about this womanfish, a creature that lived in two worlds. My girlish imagination was hooked. (And besides, her chi-chis turned me on.)

So too, was I developing a love affair with language. Fluid in both English and Spanish, I marveled at the words my mouth formed to communicate with different people in my life. There was a certain regularity in the words I used with my parents. Pero con mi abuela, the words took on a magical quality, much like her deck of cards where strange images were paired with a special language. A mermaid was simply a mermaid. To invoke her name in Spanish, however, was to transform the creature into Sirena.

From then on, I always connected Sirena with feminine space—a feeling I carried with me when I accompanied my grandmother to the homes of her many hermanas. There, amid all the familiar icons of a Mexicano household, the seven sisters would sit at the dining room table playing the game with my grandmother's deck of magic cards. High rollers that they were, the old women would throw pennies, nickels and dimes into an empty margarine tub, placing their respective bets. I loved the rough clang of the coins shaking against one another.

This mix of metals marked my first experience with alchemy.

> *Alchemy (n.)—a medieval chemical philosophy concerned primarily with the conversion of base metals into gold; a metaphor for the spiritual perfection of the soul.*

Chicana author Gloria Anzaldúa, another Tejana, speaks of alchemy as the act of making face, making soul ("haciendo caras"). As a Queer Xicana alchemist activist, I construct my soul with the raw materials of the ancients: earth, air, fire, water, and their corresponding aspects of personality. Ritually, I examine that psychic cavity where the intercourse of elements takes place. Indeed, my cultural reality demands that I never stop, for it is a simple matter of creative and political survival. Here, in this space where earth, air, fire and water consummate and consume one another, my consciousness is born, molded by The Foremother's hands.

Mujeres such as Anzaldúa have already named this volcanic creator: from Her all things come; it is She whose lava bleeds the four elements with the birth of each full moon. Spewing rock, gas, liquid flame, her cunt is a cauldron of alchemical perfection. Her power speaks to us— the daughters and the brujas—telling us stories of spiritual creation. And not unlike my own abuela, her hands hold the power to reveal those cultural archetypes so important to our lives. She acts as her own midwife, delivering from her firewomb a pantheon for a new generation of politically engaged mujeres.

Standing at the water's edge of a new millennium, we must now retell these stories of spiritual creation, the tales of how we make our souls anew.

"*La Sirena ... La Dama ... La Luna*," I remember my abuela calling out as each mysterious image met our eyes. "*El Arbol, El Diablo, El Sol ...*"

"*El Cantarito ...*"

El Cantaro, the water pitcher, was another symbol telling of spiritual creation. In this case it was my own creation: I entered life under the sign of Aquarius, the water bearer.

The sign of Aquarius is not water, but rather that of air. It is an appropriate element, for in our vases we carry the element of water, whose properties are associated with emotion. Yet as an air sign, we are creatures of the intellect. Long associated with mind and thought, the Aquarian must literally carry the waters of emotion on her back. She contains this liquid, fearful of getting wet.

An air sign given the responsibility of controlling las aguas del corazon, I stayed rational until that moonrise when I awoke with an ocean in my bed. There, returning from my childhood rousings of language, emotion and sexuality, lay my Sirena. We embraced, my tongue licking the salt from her pores. The thirst grew, and as she enticed me to drink, I brought my mouth to the edge of my own wetness. A taste. The vase spilled, and I unleashed the Rio Grande, river of my youth.

A Chicana Aquarian who has always carried the weight of a river on my back, I look to Sirena and discover the key to my spiritual and political survival. Her very existence speaks to my need for wholeness—a search integral to any paradigm of resistance I may create. As a living creature of alchemy, she coexists among water and air, emotion and intellect: she is the evolving mystical body. Seamless, my Sirena questions the dualistic thought that permeates both colonizer and the colonized. Indeed, her presence is a constant reminder of my struggles against the numerous colonizations that inhabit the collective unconscious of the brown queer. She remains, for me, the single most important archetype of this reality.

In Sirena's embrace, I may choose to be guided through the waters of memory, returning to my Atlantis/Aztlan. This politicized place of origin speaks to us as activists. We remember the utopian homeland, renewing hope for our community's possibilities. Simultaneously, we mourn The Loss. For while A(z)tlantis may be the indigenous source of our political myth and magic, our mestizo blood still circulates the white tidal wave that crushed a civilization. Hence, the paradox of Sirena's cancion—she is at once guardian and devourer of the dream.

Amidst the chaos, we too are swallowed whole, only to emerge from her fish belly. Transformed, we have moved from victim to survivor to witness, still breathing in the wake of catastrophe. Our stories become our most powerful testimony. Such testament, I believe, is the basis for the New Myth we must create if we are to flourish as a vibrant and decolonized people. The ancients called this endeavor toward wholeness the Great Work; as a modern alchemist activist, I too must invoke the journey. Soy *alchemistica*—the name I have given to any woman who engages the mystical dimension when conceiving strategies for radical political change. The role of this alche-mystic is to call attention to those spiritual elements we can mold in our quest for a better paradigm. I remain, after all, a firm advocate of the power of myth and symbol, malleable by necessity when cultural survival is concerned.

Ironically, the relatively recent conquest of Mexico by the United States has left many of us negotiating our definitions of "cultural survival." I speak here of language, and how Sirena for me has also become a metaphor for the dilemma many modern Chicanos face in their relationship with the Spanish language, itself a colonizer's tongue. For those of us born and raised in the Southwest, our remnants of the catastrophe have always been sedimentary; each layer of colonization weighs down upon the psychic terrain while a river erodes the cortex. In South Texas, where I was raised, this erosion often takes the form of historical erasure. Though the side of the mountain screams with the visual record of centuries, many of us are blinded by a mirage of political barrenness. In this environment, my early cultural consciousness was most tied to the notion of language, symbolized in many ways by La Sirena.

It has been several years since I sat as a child on the bed of my grandmother, playing a card game of words and images. My early emotional memories, such as my queer sexuality, included those that came from speaking fluently en español con mi abuela. This notion of unrestrained expression, of joyous familiarity, was soon shattered by the invisible hand of white supremacy. To this day I have never experienced a "direct" attack on my brown self and yet, as a young child, the stealth messages that Spanish equaled Mexican equaled something to be ashamed of infiltrated my young mind, causing me to ban my parents from speaking to me in a language other than English.

My entrance into the school system finalized this severance; English became the language of critical thought and analysis while Spanish—

the romantic and "irrational"—became the deprecated language of the heart. For the next several years I communicated with my grandmother in a fragmented Spanish of contained emotions. My own grandmother—the primary tie to a culturally decapitated past—died unable to fully understand the thoughts and feelings I wanted so much to share with her, because I could not speak her native tongue.

To this day I often wonder if part of my difficulty behind relearning Spanish has to do with the fact that I am not yet ready to confront the emotional flood that comes with (re)discovering one's culture. I liken this flood to the coming out process. For so long I ached to taste a woman; with this same tongue I now struggle to heal the split of my denied cultural self. My experience with this forked tongue of shame still haunts me. And as a Chicana, I know I am not alone.

Like the Little Mermaid of the folk tale, many in our culture become mute as we make the tragic pact to step on land, emulating the footsteps of Anglo colonizers. We ache to breathe the air of English, inhaling the privilege it carries. We have seen this prince of privilege from the refracted pool of history, fallen in love with a distorted view. When the fish tail is finally sacrificed and white legs walk on land—a land that once was ocean—we discover emotional indifference. The prince we search for never loved us. The attempt fails, and we are left psychically severed in two, wishing again for a tail and the fluidity it once gave us. We yearn for the emotion of home and familia. Mute and broken-hearted, the mermaid's body disintegrates into spray, returning to her native source.

I choose to believe the Little Mermaid is reborn as Sirena, an oceanic curandera singing the joys of a healing ritual. Alchemical in nature, her rites are the *prima materia* for the New Myth I must now create. This is the crux of the The Great Work. Defiant in the face of fragmentation, I fuse my political struggle with a profound sense of the sacred, speaking con cuerpo y corazon. Only then do I begin the true integration of her form. Sirena becomes my body, never to leave me again.

Go Ahead

Theresa Delgadillo

GO AHEAD, take my life. It hasn't been mine for some time anyway.

Don't mistake me—I'm not feeling sorry for myself. If I'd gotten further on the English language videos that Nicolás bought for us, I might be able to tell you this myself. I might be able to explain to each one of you, beyond a reasonable doubt as they say, that I wanted him dead.

Sandra and Carlito have learned English so fast that they could probably tell you—if I ever talked to them about what happened. But these are not matters for children. And you cannot know what I feel for my children or what I would do to protect them. It's nothing like the momentary sympathy you showed yesterday when my lawyer's hard-working-mother-driven-to-desperation speech softened you.

She's pretty good for a court-appointed attorney—better than I expected, probably better than you expected. You had a look on your faces that I'd seen before, but where? Ah, sí, the couple who brought us a box full of food one Christmas. Understand this: my children don't need your pity. There is no father more responsible than Nicolás and no mother less in need of your mercy than myself.

Do you think I don't know that underneath the designer suit or the fancy dress you're just like me? Yes. Just like me. I know that if I keep staring at you, looking at you just like this, you'll prove me right. You can hate, too. You can fear, too. You can take me away from Nicolás and our children. And you would be right.

Don't let my lawyer fool you. I knew what I was doing. I remember, even, the first time I thought about it. It was the day when the third and last working toilet backed up. He was in a frenzy, pacing up and down the aisles of the shop floor, screaming that we were animals, his hands punctuating his shouts, while we tried to hide ourselves in the hum of a hundred sewing machines.

On the loudspeaker he said, "You people disgust me! You're a bunch of dirty pigs! I can't believe I have to pay for your mess! You all just make me sick!" His mouth was a dark hole surrounded by bright teeth, and the veins in his pale throat pulsed with anger.

I was holding my shears when he began yelling, and when he finished I thought, "How I'd like to shove these right into your gut." That simple. Sure, by then, as my lawyer says here in court, I had already "exhausted other avenues of redress."

It was only a few months before that he had shouted me down in an argument over the price for welt pockets we were sewing on a new line of Liz Claiborne skirts. He said I was "ungrateful," "greedy," "didn't I know I was lucky to have a job in a recession?" Then he just walked away. The union chairlady told me to look out for him when he lost his temper.

Bestmade Fashions wasn't the only garment shop in town. I could have quit and gone to work somewhere else. They say this is a free country, after all. I didn't have to stay there. But I did, even when things started to fall apart. Not the machines, never, and business never slacked off much, but the paint continued to peel off the walls and the garbage piled up. He fired a bundle boy and then told us to clean up around our machines rather than hire a replacement. He set new prices. He yelled and swore at us for everything. And every day I went back to it, we all went back to it, I guess because we knew there really wasn't a "somewhere else."

When he threw a bundle at Rosario, who sat across the aisle from me, and knocked her out of her chair, the chairlady called the union office. They came and talked to him, and he stayed in his office for a few days after that. But Rosario wouldn't file a complaint because her application for permanent residency listed him as her employer.

The first time he touched me it was after work. I had just punched out after an hour of overtime. I warned him. I told him then that if he ever touched me again, I'd kill him. He laughed.

"Just stay out of his way," I thought. "Stay around other people. Don't let him get you alone." And that's just what I did. Until that day when he walked by my machine and said he wanted to see me in his office, NOW. Rosario looked up as he spoke, shaking her head in sympathy.

I stepped into the office, but stayed close to the door. He leaned back against his desk. He asked me why I wasn't working much overtime anymore. Said he needed me to work more. He came closer and I looked out the glass windows of his office and I could see the whole shop, and I wasn't answering, and he was saying "Maria, I'm talking to you, I need you to work more," and his face was twisting into a smile and I felt his hand grab my breast and his other hand on my thigh and I watched everybody moving on the shop floor, fabric swishing through the machines and through the air, a dance of scarves, and Rosario looking up from her machine, puzzled and then concerned, and then I felt warm liquid on me and he gasped, falling backwards, hitting his head on the desk, and through the window I could see some of the other operators looking up at me, and finally, the dance stopped.

When they pushed the door open, they shoved me forward, toward him, lying there on the floor, in a puddle of blood, my orange-handled shears stuck in his gut.

My lawyer tells me to stop staring at you, but I can see the change coming into your eyes—you will be glad never to have to see me again when this is over. Each of you will go back to work: the advertising office, the county welfare office, the classroom, the museum. You will not see me tied to the table. You will not witness the injection.

The needle does not move itself, however, and neither does the little needle on a sewing machine in a shop across town where those fancy garments that each of you wear get made. You need real human beings to move those needles. Just as you need a real human being to prepare the one that will puncture my skin. I can see now that I do not need to reassure you about this, your civic duty. You are prepared now, maybe always have been, to wield the power you have to do the right thing. So do it. Just know that you don't fool me by the clothes you wear: the Evan Picones, Carole Littles, Ralph Laurens, Donna Karans, Calvin Kleins.

Don't forget, I sewed those clothes. I know what they're made of.

Granola Whites, Polyester Indians

Gloria Dyc

"THEY'RE BUSTING PEOPLE on the land," David reported as soon as he hung up the phone. "They've got Hopi and Navajo fencers out and there are about nine guys from AIM around with weapons. That's a lot of heat." He began to thumb through the stack of phone messages that had been left for him at his Berkeley home throughout the day. This was David's routine: as soon as he arrived home from his job with the Environmental Protection Agency, he began to work with fervor for the Big Mountain Defense Committee.

His wife, Penny, did not look up from her newspaper. She was sitting at the round oak table with one leg tucked underneath her as though she anticipated that the moment of relaxation would be brief. The article she was reading, printed in one of the Bay area's alternative newspapers, was titled "Rowena: Modern Day Witch."

"Any plans for dinner?" David asked as he paced between the kitchen and the living room. "I might have to go down to the Center. This is great timing, anyway. If anything goes down, we can confront the Hopi chairman tomorrow at the press conference."
"I thought we'd just *graze*. Isn't that the new word—*graze*?" Penny asked with irony in her voice.

Dawn, Penny's teen-aged daughter, slouched in a rattan chair in the living room and played with the remote control to the television. The shows bored her, so she switched stations often. She liked to create a kaleidoscope effect by juxtaposing newscasts with rock videos, comedies and game shows.

"I'm *sick* of not having anything to eat," Dawn complained. "There's nothing to *graze* on." She hated to even look in the refrigerator. No meat, "natural foods." There were moldy packets of food which she could not identify. The vegetables had rotted into a fragrant liquid in the bin. Penny was busy with her erratic schedule as a mid-wife, and she was an inept shopper. She would buy salsa and forget the tortillas; when they had tortillas they would run out of salsa. Dawn wished her parents would eat normal food like steak. But like some other parents in the area, Penny and David were "granola people." They drove around in a twelve-year old Volvo with bumper stickers that read "Stop Contra Aid" and "U.S. Out of North America."

"So, what do you *want*?" Penny asked her daughter.
"I want a Walkman," Dawn responded. "Everyone at school has a Walkman."
"*Everyone* has one, huh?" Penny was examining the photo that went along with the modern witch article. According to the caption, the women were enacting an ancient ritual; Penny thought they looked like they were in an outdoor aerobics class.

"What were your grades, anyway?" Penny asked her daughter. "'D' in Science, 'D' in Math. What did you get in English?"
"'D' *plus*," Dawn answered sarcastically. This was not a good time to bargain for the Walkman. She hated Science. In the Science room there was a picture of the solar system with colorful spinning planets and stars. Sometimes Dawn would stare off into the chart and imagine the whole system in motion; she appreciated the order and solitude of each planet in its orbit. There seemed to be no center in their house; each person was on a separate trajectory. She turned up the volume on the television and began to change stations more quickly.

Penny took inventory of the contents of the refrigerator. "You know what's going to happen now that there's trouble down there," David said, following her into the kitchen. "The government is going to move in and say, 'We're going to move everyone out for their own protection.'"

Penny was tired of hearing about Big Mountain politics. David had promised that once the deadline for relocation had passed and there was some sort of resolution, he would slow down his political work. She wanted them to be together as a family again, to be able to take in a movie or go out to dinner.

"So, what are we going to graze on?" David asked.

"I don't know," Penny said with exasperation. "I was going to make enchiladas, but the cheese is bad. I thought I could cut the mold off, but it's *all* mold. Maybe we could go out and pick up some pasta and pesto."

David gave her an impatient look and went back to his business calls. He was updating members of the support group on the latest developments in Arizona and planning a big press conference. They would surprise the Hopi tribal chairman by bringing in a woman leader from his own tribe. She was opposed to the plan to relocate the Navajos out of an area that they have traditionally shared, but she had been unable to get an audience with the chairman.

Penny resented her husband's preoccupation with his political work, but she felt guilty because she knew they had a good life. They had a house with a sunny courtyard; if she stood on the redwood railing of the deck, she could get a glimpse of the Bay. They had money in the bank. David was in charge of monitoring air quality in Arizona, so they both had the opportunity to travel to the Southwest. They toured the Four Corners area to witness the consequences of coal mining; vast areas had been transformed into gray, lunar wasteland. The mining companies, Penny learned, have a voracious appetite for water—the water table was being depleted.

And then Penny and David had gone into the joint use area where the government was attempting to relocate the Navajo. The Navajos and Hopis had lived there together for centuries; the Navajo still tended their sheep. The conflict, some of the Indians reported, was being manufactured by the government and "greedy" tribal politicians. Penny admired the women. They were strong and centered; they laughed and were fearless. They hauled wood and built fires for cooking their cornmeal, mutton and dried beans. They knew how to handle guns. In their brightly colored skirts and velveteen blouses they would sit down in the path of government fencers, resisting each wave of encroachment on their way of life. *And here I am*, Penny thought, *pissing and moaning because I have to run down to the gourmet shop to pick up pesto and pasta!*

Penny waited for her husband to get off the phone so they could continue the meal-time negotiations. "David...maybe *you* could run out to the store. Louise may go into labor today; I'm expecting her to call. And Jane is stopping by...she had to go to the clinic to get that biopsy done." "Penny, I have a *meeting*. I'll just have to pick up something on the way."

Dawn had been listening to the latest development on the dinner situation. She went into her bedroom and flopped down on her bed. She was hungry; she couldn't stand it. "I'm sick of not having any food around here. I'm going to *kill myself*," she screamed.

Penny and David looked at one another without speaking. "What would you like, Dawn?" Penny asked in a conciliatory voice. "Stop talking *at me*, asshole," Dawn yelled back.

The phone rang and David hurried downstairs to take the call in his office. "I can't take this," Penny warned him as he fled. "We're going to have to see that therapist." David did not want to see a therapist; therapy was bourgeois and he was a busy man. All he wanted to do was relax for ten minutes, get his papers together and get to the meeting.

Jane leaned against the redwood railing of Penny's balcony, soaking up the last hours of sun. Her hair was cut short and she wore a loose, cotton outfit that could be worn by either gender. "The weather is changing. Have you noticed?" she mused. "It's *Chernobyl*. That was a huge

explosion—it had to do something. The planet is definitely *cooling off.*"
"The world is insane," Penny sighed. "Are you hungry? I was thinking about ordering out. I don't feel like cooking and my daughter is *starving* to death."
"I've been on a fast," Jane said, shaking her head. "Cleaning myself out. I'm getting the results of the biopsy tomorrow. If it's the big 'C,' they can do the surgery tomorrow." She lifted up her cotton shirt to expose her breast and began to gently feel for the lump. "It's definitely gotten bigger in the past month."

Penny joined her in the examination, moving her experienced fingers over Jane's breast. Dawn had come out of her exile in the bedroom. She was feeling apologetic after her outburst. *Oh gross,* she mumbled, as she watched the breast examination. She returned to her room, wondering why they had to be so *public* about sexuality. Penny felt the lump in her friend's breast with alarm; it was the size of a tennis ball. She gave Jane a hug.

"I don't know why they didn't tell me a year ago. That's laid-back Lake county for you," Jane complained, trying to hold back the tears. "The doctor told me it was OK and to come back in a few months." She reached into her pocket and took out a list of herbal remedies which she handed to Penny. Jane had gone to a pendulum healer and she had watched as the pendulum swung above a chart and seemed to stop, magically, over the remedies appropriate for her condition.

Penny looked at the list with a sense of foreboding; if the tumor were malignant, there would be no need for such remedies.

"And I have *these,*" Jane added with hope; she took out two crystals from her pocket.
"I could go for a *drink,*" Penny announced. She stepped into the kitchen, stunned by the size of the lump in her friend's breast, and began a search of the cupboards for a liquor bottle she had stashed away. A moth flew out; they nested among the cereal boxes and broken packages of pasta.

"I'm having a problem with my daughter," Penny told Jane in a soft voice. She held up an empty tequila bottle as evidence. "This was close to half full. I think she's been *drinking*."

"And you *didn't* at that age?" Jane retorted with a laugh. "They're funny, aren't they? The way Dawn took off when you were examining my breast. Your daughter is like mine. I was with a friend and we were talking about our sex lives, remembering past partners, getting down to some *raunchy* details. My daughter really got embarrassed."

"Yeah, they're funny," Penny sighed. *Two months and two weeks*, Penny thought, *it has been two months and two weeks since David and I have had sex.* "I can't wait until after this press conference," Penny confided to her friend. "David promised to let up. I want some kind of personal life."

"Not much *sex*, huh?" Jane quipped.

"Not much. We're just not talking. Dawn threatens to commit suicide. David hides in his office. I set up an appointment last week with a family therapist, but no one was around to go except me."

The sun was lower now and the adjacent houses cast their shadows on the deck where the women sat. Jane reached for her friend's hand and they sat quietly. Penny didn't want to dwell too much on her own situation; the possibility that her friend might have her breast removed the next day seemed so much more serious.

"I do visualization," Jane said softly. "I imagine my T-cells are like sharks, attacking invaders. I've taken enough *peyote* to be an *Indian*."

"I wonder if Rowena could do some sort of ceremony," Penny offered, though her heart was shadowed in doubt.

"*Damn* that doctor," Jane hissed. "He should have known better." Then she allowed herself to cry.

A dozen reporters had arrived on the seventh floor of the San Francisco Press Club. Members of the Big Mountain Defense Committee and the International Treaty Council were there to greet them, serve them coffee and pass out their pamphlet titled "P. L. 93-531: Justice or Genocide?" The reporters, dressed in conservative, tailored clothes, were anxious to get started on time, for they had other stories to cover, and to their minds most of those were more important than this land dispute and relocation plan in the Southwest.

Dressed in jeans and Western boots, turquoise jewelry and other ethnic clothing, the Big Mountain people were easy to distinguish from the reporters. A woman representing the International Treaty Council stood talking with several reporters. "We do not *own* the land," she was saying, "We are here as caretakers of this earth. We don't believe there's a dispute between the Hopi and Navajo; there's a dispute over what's *underneath* the land—uranium, coal, *money*. According to the U.N., the forced removal of people from the land is *genocide*." One of the reporters put his notebook in his pocket and discreetly moved away to get a cup of coffee. Genocide, he believed, occurred in Russia, Africa, Latin America—but not in the United States.

"I can't wait to see his face when he walks in," David whispered to Ruth, the Hopi leader opposed to the resolution plan. Ruth sat with complete equanimity on a couch, waiting for the Hopi chairman and his public relations coordinator to arrive. David admired her serenity. "This p.r. woman, does she have any Indian blood?" he asked. David was afraid that the chairman would bolt when he saw Ruth and realized that he had been tricked into a public confrontation with a member of his own tribe.

"Not a drop," Ruth said with a soft laugh. She never completely understood why the white people wanted to get so involved in their tribal politics, but she appreciated their help at times. "The same public relations firm represents a big coal company."

At that moment, the elevator door opened and a stark-looking woman in a black and white printed dress stepped into the foyer. With her pale skin, black hair and heavily made-up face, she appeared cadaverous. Her ankles were so slim that she appeared to be precariously balanced on her spiked heels. She was talking over her shoulder to the Hopi tribal chairman, quite a few inches shorter. The Hopi chairman saw Ruth and stopped; his eyes scanned the room, he tried to conceal the fact that he was nonplused. His hair was styled into a pompadour; his nails were freshly buffed and he wore a navy blue polyester suit. When his public relations woman realized what was going on, she pivoted awkwardly on her spiked heels, a spasm of panic on her face, and ushered the chairman back into the elevator.

David quickly pursued them. He found the p.r. woman smoking a cigarette and pacing the sidewalk in front of the press club. The chairman looked distant and uncomfortable; he took his cues from her. She admonished David for not being "above-board," for not "playing by the rules." The eyelashes of one eye, thick with mascara, stuck together for a moment and she had to separate them with her long, red nails.

David enjoyed the confrontation. His dissemblance and political maneuver were minor, he thought, compared to the tactics used by those who had real power and money. At the EPA David had acquired a reputation for conducting meetings in a "hostile" way, and that's the way he liked it. He did not joke or laugh with the corporate men; he didn't discuss sports or vacation plans. After EPA meetings, he wanted to see winners and losers, and he made that clear through his quiet strength and unwillingness to compromise.

"You'll look *worse* if you walk out," David warned the p.r. woman. Within ten minutes he had convinced them to resume the press conference.

Polyester Indians, David thought as he glanced at the nervous Hopi chairman in the elevator. This was the term that David and his friends used to refer to Indians who had assimilated into American culture. David appreciated the colors of the Southwest: the geometric designs of the hand-woven blankets, the shirts and skirts the people wore, the turquoise and silver jewelry. With such a legacy of color and natural fabrics, how could an Indian wear such an unnatural, ugly fabric?

David was equally dismayed by the fact that the chairman was a Mormon. He had sat with some of the Hopi and Navajo elders and had been honored to hear some of the old stories and teachings. Some of the Hopi prophecies had already come to pass. He remembered the words of one elder:

> Our minds are on material instead of spiritual things. If we continue to disturb nature, nature will turn its face away. The corn will say: 'We are not going to produce any more.' The apple tree won't produce fruit anymore. They are all going to turn their faces away if we neglect them. We may have a pocketful of money, but that's not going to help...

The reporters turned with restlessness and impatience as David and the chairman returned to the press conference room. David moved to the podium and introduced the speakers; Ruth was given the opportunity to speak first. She spoke without notes in a gently self-assured manner. "A couple of nights ago I met with the religious leaders. They told me to tell the people that there is no dispute between the Hopi and Navajo people. We have written our tribal chairman many letters and they have all gone unanswered..."

David looked to the back of the room: the tribal chairman was writing notes, and the public relations woman paced the floor like a basketball coach.

"I am pained that we had to come here and hash this out in front of the press," Ruth continued. "If we really believe in our grandfathers and grandmothers, we shouldn't be divided this way." Her eyes filled with tears and she stopped for a moment to collect herself. The public relations woman had the ear of a reporter in the back of the room and passed out brochures.

"If they could just leave us alone—the government—*leave us alone*," Ruth pleaded. David felt some guilt for arranging the press conference and wondered if the two could begin to talk now.

The tribal chairman took his notes and stepped up to the podium. He stated that he, too, was a traditionalist. He, too, acted only on the recommendations of his elders. As David listened it became clear that the chairman's rhetoric was similar to Ruth's, but the chairman kept reminding reporters that he was an elected official. David sensed that the reporters were shifting their interest and loyalties to the chairman.

"You have to understand that the *Navajos* started this development," the chairman responded, "They invaded our land, and now they are collecting millions of dollars a year on coal leases. We Hopi are traditionalists in our *hearts*, but we still need *income*. Our unemployment rate is 90%. Some of these *outside* agitators, who already have a high standard of living, don't understand this." He had begun to sweat; he took out a white handkerchief and blotted his forehead. The p.r. woman cupped her hands and raised them triumphantly: her team had scored. The reporters energetically took notes. Some raised their hands to eagerly ask questions.

David could predict the outcome: the Big Mountain Support Group would be depicted by the press as "outside agitators" interfering with government policy and the economic development of the Hopi. Members from another group were arriving for the next scheduled press conference. The waitresses were bringing in fresh coffee. Their press conference would have to come to an end. David walked down the stairs with Ruth, who said simply, "The elders have told us that once we learned the English language, we would turn against one another. This is part of the prophecy."

Penny arrived home from the birth at three o'clock in the morning. David had fallen asleep on the couch. The television station had gone off the air and the room crackled with static. She set about making tea, trying to keep the noise to a minimum. *I'm going to confront him*, she thought, *I'll give him an ultimatum: the marriage or Big Mountain.*

Penny was exhausted from the ordeal of the evening, but so over-stimulated she knew sleep wouldn't come easily. She sat with her tea in the kitchen and tried to figure out what clues she could use to screen out women who were not suited for home birth. Louise, her client, was forty and this had been her first delivery. She was a strict vegetarian: her refrigerator was stocked with bottled water and unfiltered fruit juices, tofu and bags of grain. But to Penny's dismay, Louise hadn't been exercising regularly. Penny explained the risks, but Louise clung stubbornly to the idea of home birth.

The condition of Louise's Napa Valley house had appalled Penny when she had arrived. Louise and her construction-worker husband had not bothered to clean: the carpet was covered with animal hair. One of the dogs was wearing a diaper, due to incontinence. *He's not in pain*, Louise had explained, *and it's so much more humane than taking him to the vet to be killed.* Penny let the dogs out of the house, noticing some feces on the carpet. Then she heard a blood-curdling scream: it was Louise.

In the bedroom, the mid-wife trainees were working with Louise—offering her encouraging words, coaching her on her breathing, rubbing her back and arms. From the trainees' facial expressions it was clear that it had been a long, difficult evening. With each contraction, Louise lost all control; her eyes dilated in horror, she looked possessed. *There must be something wrong*, she said to Penny in an accusing voice. The mid-wives shook their heads in exasperation. *The pain is natural; it's a good pain,* Penny reminded Louise. *Maybe we should go to the hospital,* Louise said in alarm. Then she howled. Penny had called the trainees into the next room for a conference.

David awoke when he heard the whistle of the tea kettle. *Jane*, he thought immediately. *I'll have to tell Penny about Jane.* He laid in the darkness of the living room, immobilized by dread. Then he went out to join her in the kitchen.

"How did the delivery go?" he asked Penny. She was startled for a moment by his sudden presence in the doorway, and when she remembered the ultimatum she wanted to deliver, her heart beat faster.

"I don't even know if I can talk about it," Penny said in disgust. "She delivered in the *hospital*, finally." Several moths flew around the kitchen. David fixed himself a cup of tea.

"Complications?"

"Yeah, Louise was a *wimp*. I've never heard anyone carry on the way she did. It was *horrible*. She was so *close*, too, after twelve hours of labor you could see the baby's head. Then she started screaming, 'Take me to the hospital.'"

The episode at the hospital had been humiliating to Penny and her assistants. A male doctor had come to the admission area and told them he would not do anything until the appropriate legal papers were signed, releasing him from responsibility. *I'm in charge now*, he said. *I make the decisions. You have three minutes to think about it.* Louise was eager to sign. She begged him for drugs and then, five minutes after the spinal, she delivered her baby.

"Do you know what Louise said?" Penny complained to David. "She said, '*Thank you*, doctor.' We had been with her for twelve hours."

"Down in the Southwest, the women go off with a mid-wife, but they don't make a sound. They have a fundamentally different view of childbirth," David mused.

"I wish I were a Navajo," Penny sighed.

"You'd better think twice about that. Things are pretty rough for them right now," David chastised. He reviewed the events of the press conference, but Penny was so exhausted she couldn't keep track. "The corporations and the government want the coal and the uranium. They want more *bombs*," he concluded bitterly.

"David, I think you're going to have to make a choice now. Between me and the politics," Penny blurted out.

"I'm not sure if I can do that, Penny," David responded with a calm detachment Penny hadn't anticipated. They sat for a moment in silence and Penny wondered if he had fallen in love with someone else. "Jane called," he said finally. Penny felt a surge of apprehension. "It's *cancer*. They opened her up, but there's not much they can do. She's filled with it, Penny; it spread to her lymph nodes."

Penny let out a moan; not her friend Jane! They had all been working, in their own way, to hold back the tidal wave of destruction—but it was too powerful. What were flower remedies and crystals in the shadow of this cancer? She wanted David to take her hand, to hold her, but she knew he would not.

As the two sat in silence at the kitchen table, an image of a street preacher came to David's mind. After the press conference, David had spent some time by himself downtown. He was near the trolley station, where tourists lined up to climb aboard the famous San Francisco attraction. At least the area was lively: a man from Jamaica played the bongos, someone passed out political leaflets. Then David saw the street preacher; he was taking advantage of a captive audience of tourists lined up for a block. His hair was white and he was wearing a blue suit and tie. His voice was histrionic, but there was a detached expression on his face, so the voice seemed to come from a recording. *Are you prepared to meet the Lord?* He held a bible in his hand and tried to make contact with individuals, but they were adept at blocking him out. *The Lord tells us what we need to do before we are saved. We need to repent now.*

Someone in the crowd mocked him and some others began to laugh. The expression of the preacher changed, as if he had just woke from a sleepwalk. *What did he say?* the preacher looked around anxiously but he could not identify the man who mocked him. *This man needs a head transplant. We ALL need head transplants.* David and others in the crowd chuckled.

And then, David remembered, the preacher looked up in the clear, blue San Francisco sky and gestured dramatically, as though the Second Coming were occurring. *Where are YOU going to be when those missiles come down?* he asked the crowd and looked around, his voice vibrating with passion. *What are you going to do when those missiles come raining down?*

July

SOME DAYS I can't get out of bed, and some days I rise before good light to wander for hours in the foothills and canyons of the mountains that rise to the north of the house. It is my fancy that the house faces south—the largest windows have a southern view of land that falls away in open miles of chaparral and grassland to the low place that must roughly parallel the invisible line where this country ends. There the ground rises again, gradually, toward San Mateo, the big mountain that dominates the horizon and is, so exotically and mysteriously, in another country. The first causes of my being lie in the antiquity of Mexico. And yet I have only come this far, just to the edge, where I look over the line with sadness and dismay, as though into a void.

I'm sometimes lonely here; days burn slowly in the desert. I wake before sunup to dry air noisy with mockingbirds, hummingbirds, and finches. Swallows graze the wet stones of the patio I've washed down before coffee. Water is artifice in June and July, before the rains come, and futile if the wind is blowing: stones dry before swallows find them, before I can contemplate what is reflected there: hollow blue sky and copper light.

"I'm lonely," I tell Seashell, my daughter, who was born and named before I was grown up. She calls from Baltimore every Sunday morning. "Hermits in the desert are lonely," she tells me. "I thought you'd sacrificed everything for the peace of a hammock and big sky. Your going back is heroic."

Well, I know one joyful thing: I no longer have a calendar; those tyrannical little squares of days written over, even into the margins with commitments three months into the future, nailed down and irrevocable. No. No. No. Here I have a house book I started the day I came. In it I record the daily making of my life in this house, but only so far as I truly have a will to make the house, and to make my own life in it.

Here I'd hoped to rediscover the clarity and incorruptibility of a childhood that is, perhaps, only imagined; to look up through branch and leaf of the cottonwood trees into infinite clear sky and try to feel even once again, a simplicity of understanding expressed in feelings like pure joy, and gratitude for the light that heats the stones of the patio; innocence.

It is in this house that I once knew the happiness of unqualified love and unconditional acceptance. I'd been born, my Mexican father's first child, into a household of blonde Swedish half-siblings. My mother kept curls of their white baby hair in a gold locket on a chain around her neck. The curls looked like angel hair, glistening and translucent. Fascinating photographs of my sisters at five and six, wearing their white-blond bangs immaculately trimmed in remarkably fastidious straight lines above enormous white-lashed blue eyes captivated me, convinced me of my innate inferiority. Weren't angels always depicted as fair and blue-eyed? In the photographs my sisters wore smocked velvet dresses with large round collars. Their white anklets, trim within black leather Mary-Janes, were smoothly turned down, pressed to pale cherubic legs. By the time I arrived, the sisters were grown girls in high school, but I heard story after story of their infallible goodness, their ability to stay clean and out of trouble; they were unimpeachable and I was foul. I pored over the pictures in the album. I looked like no one, even my Mexican father had pink skin, and his black curly hair lay back, away from his wide forehead.

I thought I looked grimy, and the mirror confirmed my opinion. I lived in a world of pastel people, and my presence was a blot on all that pink and white perfection. My Swedish mother bleached the dark peach-fuzz that grew down onto my cheeks. She tried to cut bangs at my forehead, but my hair rebelled; the widow's peak interfered and the bangs stuck straight out. The bobbing of the rest of my very straight hair didn't come off well either; my hair grows back, strongly back all around my head. On my neck, my hair grows low, almost to my shoulders, lies in a symmetrical swirl on either side, upward, toward the center of my neck. I know now that hair growing so is lovely; wisps spiraling low on the neck are embellishment, a subtle bit of ornament or bedizenment to an ordinary arrangement of hair. The hairdresser always shaved me to make a clean "neck." It made instead what I could only call a beard: short ugly stubble up into my hairline. Irresistible to touch, I couldn't keep my hands off it; it grew as quickly as the haircut was finished.

I had no peace. My mother tolerated me; I was not even a tertiary afterthought. My father was often away on business and I didn't know there was another child in the world who looked even remotely like me, or had such a horridly difficult name, impossible to say. I longed to be Carolyn Hill or Wendy Miller. In twelve years of public school, no one, teachers or students ever tried to pronounce my name correctly. All efforts on my part to correct the bungled syllables were met with even more distortions, so I gave it up and settled into elementary education as an oddity—the butt of jokes for my name, in which I only later learned to have pride—and a curiosity for my bleached facial hair, dark skin, and the beard on the back of my neck.

At the end of fifth grade, my Swedish mother flew to Goteburg, consoled by my sisters, and I drove with my Papi to the Southwest. As we rolled across the country, the sky grew wide and bright. I couldn't believe how far I could see. Clouds made colored shadows on the faraway mountains, and sunsets gold-leafed fine lines on the bottoms of purple clouds, like the gold edges of frail pages of the Bible. The landscape affected me like the idea of God Himself; it too was holy. And more, the stores and gas stations were populated with souls who looked like my father and me. Occasionally Papi spoke Spanish to a storekeeper or to someone in a restaurant. In the past, I had heard him speak that strange language only on the telephone when he was talking with his sister or his parents; now he used it like currency, and we were richer and richer for the use of it as we moved west.

Food also changed as we drove; Papi showed me how to use a tortilla to eat *los comestables*, the meat and rice and beans from my plate. He taught me Spanish words: I learned *cielo* and *montaña* and *sierra*. He taught me to say that I was very pleased to meet my grandparents and my aunt, *en español*.

The space and color of the western landscape became the expected condition of the world, and my complexion and hair were no longer a burden. I ate a sandwich at a cement table by the side of the road under the branches and leaves of a cottonwood tree beneath a blameless sky. For the first time ever, I was free of the weight of my life. I threw my head back and lived those minutes in absolute purity of consciousness. The sweet guilelessness of that time under the tree would recur again and again (on clear days under branches of innocent trees all over the world). Each time, the remembrance comforted me, but a day did come when I sat in a swing under a Live Oak sky with my baby on my knees. She was rapt, looking up, up through the branches. She smiled, then broke into a laugh. I wanted to laugh too, but when I looked up, I felt only heaviness and the weight of this life, and I knew I'd lost my innocence, and that the loss was permanent.

After innocence, joy comes from whatever we find on the shelf, from the fine things we've stored away within ourselves. The ancient Greeks had it right, *poiein*: to make. And the first thing you make is your own life; it is ultimate high art and one hasn't much time: I wasted twenty years lusting after domestic perfection. When I left Baltimore I carried away intimate knowledge of the interstices between each waxed floorboard in that old house (o god I waxed over little bits of dirt I *knew* were there); I lamented that house every day of those twenty years: that house where a spring flowed spontaneously beneath my waxed floors, and termites and carpenter bees riddled foundation and attic. The roof was mossed over, weatherworn; it leaked. I masqueraded as a cook, a cleaner, a wife and a Young-East-Coast-Matron, and I found no consolation in philosophy.

"Your neuroses are just deprived of a familiar context," Seashell says. "Even though it makes your hair flat you thrive in humidity. You will feel happier when it rains."

"I don't have neuroses, and that's official. I have mild anxiety. But you're right about the rain." Seashell's voice falls into my ear each Sunday morning like notes from a music box or a wind chime. I hear her husband Mike puttering in the background. Mike and I communicate through the medium of Seashell, the beloved we hold in common. He tells her to tell me "Hi," and sometimes (I think grudgingly), "Love." My child is Seashell only to me, has been Suzanne since she was four, a name she chose herself. "At least," she says, "you weren't specific, didn't name me Scotch Bonnet, or Conch."

No. And I didn't call you Lorenza or Graciela, or Xica, or any other name that would fall on ears tone deaf to the sounds of the Spanish and Indian tongues. These are my thoughts; they would not translate over satellites or through miles of telephone wire except to make me sound sullen or moody, which today anyway, I am not.

Suzanne is blonde like her father, which was a shock when she began to shape up. Her baby hair came in not black or brown, but in fine wisps of pale blonde, recalling sharply those bits of fluff in my mother's locket. Suzanne's skin went from afterbirth red to pink, and stayed that way. Her eyes stayed blue. What happened? I thought dark people were genetically dominant. I wondered if she'd been switched in the hospital, but the truth is, she *does* look like me, some; she looks like both her parents, as she should. I stayed in the east to raise my blonde child. She would grow up in densities of towns and cities, spend summers on eastern beaches with little friends named Hilary and Michele, Toby and

Peter. Though I took her west, introduced her to our Southwestern heritage, her real life is in Baltimore. She was raised looking up through locust and maple trees there, was loved there.

What more satisfying existence could I construct than what I've made here so far, a coincidence of solitude and peace, a garden inside the cracked walls, my books and music, the infinitely changing light on the mountains? And just over there, Mexico. I am lying in a hammock stretched between two mesquite trees, watching the mountain. When my grandmother died, she left the house to me. There was no one else waiting in line; my father died in the late seventies, and my beautiful Mexican Tía Elena and *mi abuelo* Lorenzo died together in a car crash in the blowing sands of southeastern Arizona twenty-eight years ago.

I've been here a year. Since January, there has been no rain; only mercilessly blue sky. Of course, I often think of my life in Maryland, and seasons. When I left there, I thought I was leaving it behind, had finished with it, especially the climate: the east coast would subside as the desert tide rose. But memory is strong for Baltimore; I lived there too many years. Each day I survey the desert for skies arched over with the miserable promise of a three-week downpour, for the discontent of an isolated thunderstorm, for the affliction of a lightning strike. I want to skid over pavements greased with rain.

In southern Arizona, it rains in summer, and I'm impatient for the monsoon torrents of August, for an indulgence of water, a baptism that will roister over rocks and swell profluent down the mountainside, roll through the rubble of the canyon floor and flood into the gutter stream that flows past my bedroom window. This is not the childhood summer I treasured. Then I valued each day of infinite blue, dry heat that mandated filling the decaying old cement pool my grandfather built in the twenties.

It *will* be easier when the rains begin; nothing is farther from the pith of a dry stream bed, from the restlessness of sere blue. A sky stagnant with clear has none of the virulence of hydraulics; I shun the blue, pray for rain. And it will rain.

It is raining in Mexico. Over there lightning is arcing down from purple clouds that dwarf the mountain. Above the clouds the sky is bright and blue, a perspective that will soon be lost to me as the storm moves this way. Wind is ruffling the leaves of the mesquite, and the freshening sweetness of first rain on the dust of the desert floor has overblown me; a wash of nostalgia for an irreproachable childhood afternoon passed here a long, long, time ago.

I squint into the distance at a world that only seems far away; Mexico through my eyelashes, out of focus through the rain falling in a wide gray scrim hanging limply from the cloud. The little town: houses, shops, the wide avenue, the railyard, the green fields and silver ponds of outlying farms all glint like shards of glass in the needle shafts of light which pierce the thunderhead.

The wind is higher now, and lightning is striking this side of the mountain, this side of the border. The horses are under the brush arbor and the dogs are under the beds. I'll lie here a few more minutes beneath the spectacle of rain, the danger of lightning.

~ ~ ~

August

It is raining, a soft drizzle from a high, evenly gray sky, quite unlike the usual monsoon, and it is cool. Friends in the east don't believe me when I say I sleep under blankets in August, think I'm unwilling to admit the mistake I made, defecting to what they imagine to be an impoverished landscape languishing under an ungodly sun.

This morning I made sofa pillows from remnants of a threadbare Kazak I found a few weeks ago, going to dry-rot in the rafters of the garage. I made pillow-backs from red silk shantung and corded the edges with silk rope I bought in Tucson for twenty-five dollars a yard. Two scorpions fell out of the rug when I unfolded it in the garage; desert insects who skittered into the shadows before I could obey the impulse to step on them. They belong here, the way I do, by right of inheritance.

When I arrived here with my father, that summer in the mid-50's, my Tía Elena took me in her arms. She stroked my poor bristling neck and whispered in my ear, "We'll never let them cut your beautiful hair again." Beautiful hair. No one had ever called anything of mine beautiful. I was hers then; our unity was absolute. I thought I looked just like Elena; when we stood side by side looking into the mirror, it was obvious. I was elated. We spent the summer dreaming in hammocks under the trees, talking and reading. We swam in the old pool, and when my skin became even browner, I was proud. Elena told me stories from her childhood of tricks the devil could play, and the reason there are turtles. She showed me pictures of her beautiful *esposo*, Guillermo, who had been killed, a soldier for the U.S. Army in Korea.

When I went back to Maryland in September, I took with me an incomplete but growing vocabulary and grammar of the Spanish language. I took also an insatiable taste for *chilis, frijoles, pozole,* and *menudo blanco sonorense*. And a love for Elena that was the embodiment of devotion.

And always in my possession, a small green leather handbag with a long strap so that I could wear it crossed over my body, stuffed with hair ribbons and flexible hairbands so that I could sweep my hair back from my face and neck. Elena had also showed me how to make braids. My neck was never shaved again.

I left Arizona with my sense of self as a Mexican person intact. It sustained me to understand that a large part of the world was Hispanic.

I felt cossetted by a landscape I had come to love, and for which my passion continued huge and wide within me as leaves turned and rivers froze in the Maryland landscape. I belonged in a place even more real, it now seemed, than the beautiful Maryland countryside. I have walked around ever since, holding secreted within myself the warmth of that summer. It saved my life, and continues to redeem my existence.

There are family stories about my grandfather riding his horse into this living room through the French windows. To show machismo? to impress the hands? out of sheer buffoonery? Did it upset my grandmother? I can imagine horses in here; if the act was cruel, intending chaos and a show of power, it must have been magnificent as well, shod hooves clanging on the slates of the floor, their own kind of elegance wrought from my grandfather's eccentricity. Or maybe my grandmother enjoyed the extravagance of horses in the drawing room. I would, on occasion. The rich fact of her life in this house impregnates my imagination, and these are my thoughts as I sew pillows out of what was probably my grandmother's rug.

I still have not crossed the border into Sonora. In stores I hear the local people alternately speaking English and Spanish, and it thrills me, that comfort of the border, facility and smoothness of code switching, crossing back and forth, Spanish to English, English to Spanish. I understand about half of the Spanish, but my tongue is paralyzed when I try to speak. I have determined to study the language as soon as I can find a native teacher, but the prospect scares me. Though I didn't grow up here, the time I did spend here marked me and claimed me. I grew up outside Mexican culture, an alien being in this beloved place, and I feel stunted or stopped, as if my facility for speaking Spanish had been ripped from my body when I was a child; as though some language growth hormone had been prevented from its surge into my spirit at the intended time, and left me forever dumb in my natural tongue.

~ ~ ~

September

I am definitely still an outsider here, a *gringa*, a woman without road-maps or signposts to point the way. I study Spanish, and my teacher, Mimi, is becoming a friend. Perhaps I will go to live across the border for a few years. Maybe I will simply achieve peace within myself, will accept myself for the odd person out I seem to be; I have never met another person with this same cross-cultural distress. But I am happy here. I wake happy most mornings, and no longer feel the depression that once kept me in bed. I thank the light for this, thank the space, and the distant mountains I can see, and know are easily sixty miles from my door.

Storms have come; a fine monsoon season filled with humidity to irrigate my words and break down resistance to memories that are all around me here.

"Tell me about them. Tell me about Elena and Guillermo, about your Papi and the Swedish sisters and my grandmothers. May I come to stay with you in the rain? Will you tell me their stories?" Seashell will come tomorrow afternoon, another freshet out of the clouds.

This house is constructed of the firm objects of the past; it requires submission to its reliquary nature. Tonight I will meditate long on light, on landscape, will lie quietly in my Tía Elena's bed where her dreams and memories, and the unseen lives laid away for so many years in time's attics and storehouses, wait for us. I feel tremors of their restlessness, flutters of agitation and disquiet as they acknowledge our presence and anticipate our fervent wish that they live again.

Sharon Creeden left law practice in 1983 to become a storyteller and writer. At first, she only told stories to her local storytelling group and wrote in her journal. Currently, Sharon travels the country giving workshops and concerts; last year she told stories to kindergartens on a New Mexico pueblo and to trial attorneys on a Wyoming ranch. Her first book, *Fair is Fair: World Folktales of Justice,* was awarded the 1995 Aesop Award by the American Folklore Society. Sharon divides her time between Seattle and Arizona. "In the summer, I look out on Puget Sound and downtown Seattle; in the winter I look out on the Santa Rita mountains and the desert. Just a perfect combination." She and her husband move with two cats and a laptop Macintosh filled with her story collections and book manuscripts.

Lyndsey Cronk, along with her husband and dog, recently moved to Utah after a four-year stay in San Francisco, the city she truly left her heart in. In an ongoing attempt to keep life interesting, she started a floral business called *Violets are Blue,* took a small role in a feature film, did freelance work as a corporate event coordinator, backpacked in the red rock deserts of southern Utah as often as her schedule permitted and enrolled in a few writing and photography classes. She prefers to consider herself a jack-of-quite-a-few-trades rather than a person-who-can't-stick-to-any-one-thing, and counts her writing as the most meaningful personal discovery of her life. Lyndsey's trips to the desert, although few, have yielded rich and life-changing experiences, and she has found that just knowing the desert is "there" sustains her.

Theresa Delgadillo has a Master of Fine Arts in Creative Writing from Arizona State University, and is currently enrolled in the Ph.D. program in Literature at the University of California, Los Angeles. Her publications include "My Face," a poem in the Fall 1993 issue of *Myriad,* and "Gender at Work in Laguna Coyote Tales" in the Spring 1995 issue of *Studies in American Indian Literatures.*

Sharon Matthews DiMaria grew up in Albuquerque and received her M.A. from the University of New Mexico. Her poems have appeared in *Poets On:*, *Yellow Silk*, *San Marcos Review*, and *Rio Grande Writers Quarterly*. She taught English at the University of New Mexico and the University of Georgia and directed equal-access services at UNM-Valencia in Tomé, New Mexico. She currently teaches part-time, writes, and lives in Albuquerque.

Gloria Dyc is a poet and fiction writer who lives in Continental Divide, New Mexico. Her work has been featured most recently in *Yellow Silk* and *Yefief*. Dr. Dyc is an associate professor in the English-Communications Department at The University of New Mexico-Gallup Campus.

Carla Jean Eardley is a published writer and illustrator, with credits in nationally circulated journals such as *Potpourri*, *Fennel Stalk*, *Magic Realism*, *Messages From the Heart*, *Dreams and Nightmares*, and regular contributions to Saturday Afternoon's annual anthologies of West Coast writers. She is the author and illustrator of *Your Story: A Writing Guide to Genealogists*, released in 1993 by Heritage Books, and in 1995 she received the Pickard Award for Short Fiction for her short story "Let the Reptile Judge." She lives in Tucson, Arizona, where she teaches writing and poetry for Pima Community College and Pima County Adult Education, and does layout and illustration for a variety of book-length projects.

Elizabeth Ann Galligan is a New Mexican who teaches, writes, loves conversation, and watches birds. Her ties to the Southwest and its diverse people are long and deep. She has won prizes for haiku in English and currently teaches at Adams State College in Alamosa, Colorado.

Alicia Z. Galván resides in San Antonio, Texas where she is a pharmacist and co-owns a pharmacy with her husband. She is widely involved as editor and contributor to several writers' groups, including the International Women's Writing Guild, the San Antonio Writers Guild, and Alamo Writers Unlimited. Her recent publications include three poetry collections, *Eclipse* (1996), *Enigma* (1995) and *Parenthesis* (1994); she was editor of *A Fountain of Words*, an anthology of Alamo Writers Unlimited. Her Spanish-language poetry has also appeared in

Al Principio (Southwest Texas State University, 1994 and 1995), and she was resident poet of *El Continental*, a Spanish-language weekly newspaper in San Antonio.

Maria Teresa Garcia is an anthropologist by training, an archaeologist by profession, and a writer by nature. She grew up in south Texas, studied in Mexico and Canada, and now lives in Taos with her two beautiful daughters and her husband. She feels northern New Mexico is where she is meant to be.

Rita Garitano is the author of *Rainy Day Man* (W.W. Norton, 1985) and numerous contributions to poetry and fiction anthologies, including most recently "Olivia" in *Walking the Twilight: Contemporary Fiction by Southwestern Women Writers* (Northland, 1994). Her contribution to this volume, "The Good Daughter," is a chapter from her forthcoming novel *Speedway Boulevard*. She is also currently rewriting her novel *A Spiritual Animal*, which she researched in France and Switzerland in 1990 with a grant from the Arizona Commission on the Arts. In 1992 she chose early retirement from her long-time employment as a high school teacher of Creative Writing and English in order to devote herself to writing full-time.

Jessica Jaramillo is a Chicana writer who has lived in Tucson, Arizona all her life. She is currently pursuing a degree in Creative Writing. Jessica finds the little things in life, such as the ear-splitting sounds of the Chicharra, worthy of mention. She tries to incorporate every aspect of her surroundings and heritage into her work.

Glenda Stewart Langley is thirty-nine years old and is originally from South Dakota. She has degrees in English from Northern State University in Aberdeen, South Dakota, and Texas A&M in Kingsville. Glenda has been married to Christopher Langley for fifteen years. She has published numerous poems in various collections around the country, most recently *The Rio Grande Review* and *Gypsy*. She is the author of a novella about three women in the life of a young man who gets mixed up in the militia movement. She currently teaches freshman writing at New Mexico Tech in Socorro, New Mexico, as well as a pre-college writing class at the University of New Mexico-Valencia Campus in Los Lunas.

Carmela Delia Lanza has had her poetry published in several journals including *The Blue Mesa Review*, *The Taos Review*, *New Mexico Humanities Review*, *Rio Grande Review*, *Turnstiles*, *Conditions*, *The Worcester Review*, *la bella figura* and others. Her chapbook, *Long Island Girl*, was published in 1993 by malafemmina press.

Maria L. Leyba was born to a Mexican mother and a detribalized Apache father into the Hispanic Barrio of Barelas in Albuquerque, New Mexico, where she still resides in the family home with her 19 year old daughter and 22 year old son. As a young child, she spent six years living on the New Mexico State Penitentiary grounds near Santa Fe, New Mexico. Her father was the head cook for over twenty years and was provided with housing. She has worked as a preschool teacher for over ten years. Recently she had one of her short stories turned into a drama, directed by Cecelia Aragon with La Casa Teatro and The Center for Regional Studies in Albuquerque. It was a series of dramatic monologues by and about Chicanas titled *Mas/Caras*. Maria also enjoys doing poetry performances in Albuquerque coffee houses, book stores, and galleries.

Evamaria Lugo writes: "I am a hispanic lesbian artist living and working in Tucson, Arizona. After a childhood of many places and many schools my parents decided to retire in Arizona. I have a BFA from the University of Arizona. Libraries are my temples. As a self-proclaimed 'native' I have adopted many coffee shops where I can often be found talking to friends or scribbling notes and working on my drawings. I want my work to portray everyday life as it relates to the human condition with respect, honor, and dignity. My most ardent daily prayer is that all sentient beings find happiness."

Sherry Luna was born to Peggy Ann Finchum and Gilbert Luna. She lives in the Patagonia Mountains near the U.S.-Mexican border in Arizona. She writes: "I can never stay away from the Southwest for very long. Something about the vast openness and the searing clarity of light. Too, I love the confluence of cultures along the border—the swirling and churning as religions, languages and environments come together, sometimes gracefully, sometimes violently."

Judith McDaniel is a writer and activist who lives in Tucson, Arizona. Her first visit to the Southwest was when she sat in on the trials of Sanctuary Movement workers in Tucson in 1986. That visit resulted in a book of poetry and essays, *Sanctuary: A Journey* (Firebrand). She kept visiting the Southwest and moved to Tucson in 1992 with her partner Jan. Together they hike the Grand Canyon at least once a year. The southwest desert and canyons have become home in a spiritual as well as physical sense. Her other books include *The Lesbian Couples Guide* (HarperCollins), two novels *Just Say Yes* (Firebrand) and *Yes I Said Yes I Will* (Naiad), and a book of her own poems, *Metamorphosis*. She is working on *The Life of Barbara Deming* and she is the literary executor of Barbara Deming's estate. She has also edited a volume of Deming's poetry, *I Change, I Change* (New Victoria).

Dolissa Medina, a *(Xican)alchemistica* of the South Texas variety, lives in San Francisco. She is interested in the pre-millennial reinterpretation of myths, symbols and archetypes, and is currently writing a book on the subject.

Jacqueline D. Moody was raised in South Texas and Southwest Alaska and currently resides in San Antonio. She is a full-time college student and part-time poet and waitress. She plans to continue writing as a career after graduation, and is currently working on a collection of her poetry for publication. Aside from local and school publications, "Moving Towards Morning" is her first national publication.

Jill A. Oglesby was born in Albuquerque, New Mexico. She currently teaches freshman composition at New Mexico Tech in Socorro, New Mexico, and lives in Los Lunas, New Mexico with her dogs "Ta" and "Blessing."

Antonia Quintana Pigno is from Albuquerque, New Mexico and has three private press books printed by the Zauberberg Press in Coffeyville, KS. Her work has appeared in various literary magazines, including *Kenyon Review, Ploughshares, Kansas Quarterly*, and *Cyphers* (Dublin, Ireland). In 1991, she was one of three finalists in the Barnard New Women's Poetry Series. She has had poetry residencies at Yaddo and MacDowell Colony.

Susan Chamberlin Quick was born and raised in Washington, D.C., graduated in French from Trinity College in 1970, and has lived in several different parts of the U.S. and in England. In the early 1970's, she was on the staff of the *Gillette (Wyoming) News Record* as a contributing columnist and editorial cartoonist. She has had her poetry published in magazines, and in one writing conference anthology of Wyoming poets. She has written short stories, essays, song lyrics, satire, and children's books—but her first love is poetry. She is currently finishing coursework towards a Master's Degree in Library Science. She has lived in the Southwest for five years.

The anglos in **Lorraine Ray's** family have been in Tucson more than a hundred years and the mexicans longer. Like the thoughts expressed by the dying writer in an early version of *The Snows of Kilimanjaro*, she hopes to write well of the place where she was a child.

J.M. Kore Salvato writes: "It seems funny to say something flat out here in these notes about myself and my thinking since I'm so used to giving all this work to the characters to do. Today I think of a story like a dream in which everything is an aspect of the dreamer: the sky, the old cars, the anguish of a vet peeling away layers of illusion, the ground underfoot. In 1953 I was born in western New York in town called Canandaigua on a lake by that name. I still dream about that lake even here in Tucson, Arizona, where I live now with my husband and our young daughter. During the year, I edit, teach and write, and during the summer I work in a private archive near Paris. The light is what I mention most about living in Tucson. The quality of the light here opens your eyes to things."

Susan San Miguel holds a B.A. and an M.A. in English from the University of Texas at San Antonio and teaches writing at San Antonio College. She is currently writing a novel, *The Snake Woman*.

Margo Tamez, a Mexic-Amerindian of Nde-Dne, Coahuilteco and Spanish ancestry,was born in Austin, Texas and raised in South Texas by her parents, Eloisa Garcia Tamez of Calaboz and Luis Carrasco Tamez of Premont. She is an MFA candidate in Poetry at Arizona State University. Her poetry has most recently appeared in *Americas Review, Hayden's Ferry Review, Hawaii Pacific Review,* and is forthcoming in *American Poetry Review* as well as in *Entre Guadalupe Y Malinche: A Tejana Anthology of Literature and Art.* She lives and writes from the family farm, with her husband and two babies, in rural Arizona.

Laura Tohe grew up on the Navajo reservation in New Mexico and Arizona. Her recent publications are included in *Blue Dawn, Red Earth, Returning the Gift, Callaloo,* and *Esuaires Revue Culturelle.* She is the author of *Making Friends with Water.* She has also written a children's play called *The Story of Me* for the Emmy Gifford Children's Theatre in Omaha, Nebraska. She states that when she creates, she never does it alone; there is always a creative force helping her, guiding her, because humans are not perfect. In her writing, place/home are important ingredients: she couldn't write if she didn't have a sense of place where she can imagine poems and stories happening. She is Assistant Professor at Arizona State University, and is the mother of two boys.

Freelance writer, peace activist and teacher **Emilie Vardaman** has been living in the desert for most of the last twenty five years. It was the desert's beauty and magic that inspired her to quit her teaching job and move to the Southwest. Today, she is co-owner and manager of a late night coffeehouse that provides space for emerging and professional poets, musicians and other artists. She lives with her husband on forty acres, where they use solar generated electricity, a composting toilet and water catchment.

Maria-Elena Wakamatsu : Growing up along the U.S./Mexico border gives birth to a state of mind where rules are fluid and sometimes suspended altogether for the sake of survival. Isolated from the rest of the country—from social and cultural happenings, politics, art—everything, then, becomes fair game and dehumanized, we devolve into a breed that neither side claims as one of theirs. In this selection, the author discovers that her lack of connectedness to a homeland is at the root of her lack of connectedness to others. The daughter of a Japanese father and a Mexican mother, Wakamatsu writes from the border between hemispheres, between patterns of discourse, between 1st and 3rd worlds. A hybrid, indeed, she writes from the place where they converge, create tension, and produce a new voice. The author was born in Mexico and grew up in the Yuma, Arizona area. She graduated from Arizona State University and currently resides in Tucson, Arizona.

Lorenza de Zavala-Wheeler is a fifth generation Tejana, a Texan of Mexican heritage. She presently lives in Bisbee, Arizona with her husband and cat, in a house from which she can see the entire length of the ugly brown fence that separates Naco, Sonora, from Naco, Arizona.

About the Editor

Caitlin L. Gannon was born and grew up in Santa Fe, New Mexico. This unusual place, a combination New Age mecca, cosmopolitan arts scene and tricultural small town, is where she formed her first version of reality. Northern New Mexico has always been her spiritual home, and she returns as often as possible to hike in the Pecos Wilderness, look out on the breathtaking expanse of the Galisteo basin, and explore rural county roads. Gannon received an M.A. in German Literature from the University of Arizona, and has studied Comparative Literature, Political Science and Women's Studies at the University of Bonn, Germany and Emory University. She currently makes her home among ocotillo and pomegranate trees in Tucson, Arizona, where she devotes as much of her time as she can to reading new books, writing, and being outside.

Javelina Press, founded in 1995, publishes women's fiction and nonfiction writing, focusing on new work that challenges convention and presents readers with alternative ways of understanding and experiencing the world.

Acknowledgments

"Patchwork Life" © 1997 by Sharon Creeden.

"Fertile Ground" © 1997 by Lyndsey Cronk.

"Go Ahead" © 1997 by Theresa Delgadillo.

"Deglazing the Pan" © 1997 by Sharon DiMaria.

"Granola Whites, Polyester Indians" © 1997 by Gloria Dyc.

"The Woman Who is Part Horse" © 1997 by Carla Jean Eardley.

"A Chant for Remembrance" © 1997 by Elizabeth Ann Galligan.

"Vegetables" © 1997 by Alicia Z. Galván.

"Recamara Mexicana" © 1997 by Maria Teresa Garcia.

"The Good Daughter" © 1997 by Rita Garitano.

"Los Tucsonenses" © 1997 by Jessica Jaramillo.

"Cooking Beans" © 1997 by Glenda Stewart Langley.

"Grace" © 1997 by Carmela Delia Lanza.

"Emergence" © 1997 by Maria Leyba.

"The Last Supper" © 1997 by Maria Leyba.

"Light at Dusk" © 1997 by Evamaria Lugo.

"The Bad Egg" © 1997 by Sherry Luna.

"Grand Canyon" © 1997 by Judith McDaniel.

"Ondas on Her Tongue" © 1997 by Dolissa Medina.

"Moving Towards Morning" © 1997 by Jacqueline D. Moody.

"Way Back on Solano Street" © 1997 by Jill A. Oglesby.

"En Busca de los Niños" © 1997 by Antonia Quintana Pigno.

"Sorting Burdens" © 1997 by Susan Chamberlin Quick.

"Some Familiar Artifacts of the Southwest" © 1997 by Lorraine Ray.

"Salvage Yard" © 1997 by J. M. Kore Salvato.

"Papá Sits Outside" © 1997 by Susan San Miguel.

"The Sacred Papers of Guerrero Pueblo" © 1997 by Margo Tamez.

"Riding Home" © 1997 by Laura Tohe.

"Salt River" © 1997 by Laura Tohe.

"View From the Deck" © 1997 by Emilie Vardaman.

"Russian Wedding" © 1997 by Maria-Elena Wakamatsu.

"I begin the second year in my Grandmother's house" © 1997 by Lorenza de Zavala-Wheeler.

Southwestern Women: A Bibliography

For readers interested in further exploring this subject, the following bibliography includes sources of literature, essays and history by and about Southwestern women. This is intended to be an introduction rather than a complete reference; I encourage readers to add their own favorite books to the list.

Allen, Paula Gunn. *Grandmothers of the Light: A Medicine Woman's Sourcebook* (Boston: Beacon Press, 1991); *Spider Woman's Granddaughters* (Boston: Beacon Press, 1989); *Skins and Bones: Poems 1979-1987* (Albuquerque: West End Press, 1988); *The Sacred Hoop: Recovering the Feminine in American Indian Traditions* (Boston: Beacon Press, 1986).

Anzaldúa, Gloria, editor. *Making Face, Making Soul=Haciendo Caras: Creative and Critical Perspectives by Women of Color* (San Francisco: Aunt Lute, 1990).

Anzaldúa, Gloria. *Borderlands—La Frontera: The New Mestiza* (San Francisco: Spinsters/Aunt Lute, 1987).

Austin, Mary. *The Land of Journey's Ending* (New York, London: Century Co., 1924); *The Land of Little Rain* (Boston: Houghton Mifflin, 1903).

Babcock, Barbara and Nancy Parezo, eds. *Daughters of the Desert: Women Anthropologists and the Native American Southwest, 1880-1980* (Albuquerque: University of New Mexico Press, 1988).

Beecher, Maureen Ursenback and Lavina Fielding Anderson, eds. *Sisters in Spirit: Mormon Women in Historical and Cultural Perspective* (Urbana: University of Illinois Press, 1987).

Cabeza de Baca, Fabiola. *We Fed Them Cactus* (Albuquerque: University of New Mexico Press, 1979 [1954]).

Castillo, Ana. *Massacre of the Dreamers: Essays on Xicanisma* (Albuquerque: University of New Mexico Press, 1994); *So Far From God* (New York: W.W. Norton, 1993); *My Father Was a Toltec* (Albuquerque: West End Press, 1988); *The Mixquiahuala Letters* (Binghamton, N.Y.: Bilingual Press/Editorial Bilingüe, 1986).

Cather, Willa. *Death Comes for the Archbishop* (New York: Knopf, 1957 [1927]); *The Professor's House* (New York: Knopf, 1925); *The Song of the Lark* (Boston, New York: Houghton Mifflin Company, 1915).

Cervantes, Lorna Dee. *From the Cables of Genocide: Poems on Love and Hunger* (Houston: Arte Publico, 1991); *Emplumada* (Pittsburgh: University of Pittsburgh Press, 1981).

Chavez, Denise. *Face of an Angel* (New York: Farrar, Straus and Giroux, 1994); *The Last of the Menu Girls* (Houston: Arte Publico, 1986).

Church, Peggy Pond. *House at Otowi Bridge: The Story of Edith Warner and Los Alamos* (Albuquerque: University of New Mexico Press, 1973 [1960]).

Cisneros, Sandra. *Loose Woman: Poems* (New York: Knopf, 1994); *Woman Hollering Creek and Other Stories* (New York: Random House, 1991); *My Wicked, Wicked Ways* (Bloomington, IN: Third Woman Press, 1987); *The House on Mango Street* (Houston: Arte Publico, 1985).

Coleman, Jane Candia. *Discovering Eve: Short Stories* (Athens, OH: Swallow Press/ Ohio University Press, 1993); *Shadows in My Hands: A Southwestern Odyssey* (Athens, OH: Swallow Press, 1993); *Stories from Mesa County* (Athens, OH: Swallow Press/ Ohio University Press, 1991).

Comer, Suzanne, ed. *Common Bonds: Stories By and About Modern Texas Women* (Dallas: Southern Methodist University Press, 1990).

Del Castillo, Adelaida, ed. *Between Borders: Essays on Mexicana/Chicana History* (Encino, CA: Floricanto, 1990).

Deutsch, Sarah. *No Separate Refuge: Culture, Class and Gender on an Anglo-Hispanic Frontier in the American Southwest, 1880-1940* (New York: Oxford University Press, 1987).

Drumm, Stella, ed. *Down the Santa Fe Trail and into Mexico: The Diary of Susan Shelby Magoffin, 1846-1847* (Lincoln: University of Nebraska Press, 1982 [1962]).

Elsasser, Nan, Kyle MacKenzie and Yvonne Tixier y Vigil. *Las Mujeres: Conversations from a Hispanic Community* (Old Westbury, N.Y.: Feminist Press, 1980).

Escamill, Edna. *Daughter of the Mountain* (San Francisco: Aunt Lute, 1991).

Gomez-Vega, Ibis. *Send My Roots Rain* (San Francisco: Aunt Lute, 1991).

Harjo, Joy. *In Mad Love and War* (Middleton, Conn: Wesleyan University Press, 1990); *Secrets From the Center of the World* (Tucson: University of Arizona Press, 1989); *She Had Some Horses* (New York: Thunder's Mouth, 1983).

Henderson, Alice Corbin. *The Sun Turns West* (Santa Fe: Rydal Writers Editions, 1933); *The Turquoise Trail: An Anthology of New Mexico Poetry* (Boston: Houghton Mifflin, 1928).

Hogan, Linda. *Red Clay: Poems and Stories* (Greenfield Center, NY: The Greenfield Review Press, 1991); *Mean Spirit* (New York: Atheneum, 1990).

Jaramillo, Cleofas. *Shadows of the Past/Sombras del Pasado* (Santa Fe: Seton Village Press, 1941).

Jensen, Joan and Darlis Miller. *New Mexico Women: Intercultural Perspectives* (Albuquerque: University of New Mexico Press, 1986).

Kelley, Jane Holden. *Yaqui Women: Contemporary Life Histories* (Lincoln: University of Nebraska Press, 1978).

Kingsolver, Barbara. *Pigs in Heaven* (New York: HarperCollins, 1993); *Another America/Otra America* (Seattle: Seal Press, 1992); *Animal Dreams* (New York: HarperCollins, 1990); *Holding the Line: Women in the Great Arizona Mine Strike of 1983* (Ithaca, N.Y.: ILR Press, 1989); *The Bean Trees* (New York: Harper & Row, 1988).

Kolodny, Annette. *The Land Before Her: Fantasy and Experience of the American Frontiers, 1630-1860* (Chapel Hill: University of North Carolina Press, 1984).

Lowell, Susan. *Ganado Red: A Novella and Stories* (Minneapolis: Milkweed Editions, 1988).

Luhan, Mabel Dodge. *Edge of Taos Desert: An Escape to Reality* (New York: Harcourt, Brace & Co., 1937).

Mairs, Nancy. *Plaintext* (Tucson: University of Arizona Press, 1986); *Ordinary Time: Cycles in Marriage, Faith and Renewal* (Boston: Beacon Press, 1993).

Martin, Patricia Preciado. *El Milagro and Other Stories* (Tucson: University of Arizona Press, 1996); *Songs My Mother Sang to Me: An Oral History of Mexican-American Women* (Tucson: University of Arizona Press, 1992).

Martinez, Demetria. *Mother Tongue* (Tempe: Bilingual Press, 1994).

McMillan, Terry. *Waiting to Exhale* (New York: Viking, 1992).

Mock, Charlotte. *Bridges: New Mexico Black Women, 1900-1950* (Albuquerque: New Mexico Commission on the Status of Women, 1985).

Moore, Alison. *Synonym for Love* (San Francisco: Mercury House, 1995); *Small Spaces Between Emergencies: Stories* (San Francisco: Mercury House, 1992).

Mora, Pat. *Agua Santa: Holy Water* (Boston: Beacon Press, 1995); *Nepantla: Essays from the Land in the Middle* (Albuquerque: University of New Mexico Press, 1993); *Communion* (Houston: Arte Publico, 1991); *Borders* (Houston: Arte Publico, 1986).

Naranjo-Morse, Nora. *Mud Woman: Poems From the Clay* (Tucson: University of Arizona Press, 1992).

Nathan, Debbie. *Women and Other Aliens: Essays from the U.S-Mexico Border* (El Paso: Cinco Puntos Press, 1991).

Norwood, Vera and Janice Monk, eds. *The Desert is No Lady: Southwestern Landscapes in Women's Writing and Art* (New Haven: Yale University Press, 1987).

Otero-Warren, Nina. *Old Spain in Our Southwest* (Chicago: Rio Grande Press, 1962 [1936]).

Perrone, Bobette, Henrietta Stockel and Victoria Krueger. *Medicine Women, Curanderas and Women Doctors* (Norman: University of Oklahoma Press, 1989).

Poling-Kempes, Lesley. *The Harvey Girls: Women Who Opened the West* (New York: Paragon House, 1989).

Rebolledo, Tey Diana and Eliana S. Rivero, eds. *Infinite Divisions: An Anthology of Chicana Literature* (Tucson: University of Arizona Press, 1993).

Rose, Wendy. *Bone Dance: New and Selected Poems, 1965-1993* (Tucson: University of Arizona Press, 1994).

Silko, Leslie Marmon. *Yellow Woman and a Beauty of the Spirit: Essays on Native American Life Today* (New York: Simon & Schuster, 1996); *Sacred Water: Narratives and Pictures* (Tucson: Flood Plain Press, 1993); *Almanac of the Dead* (New York: Simon & Schuster, 1991); *Ceremony* (New York: Viking, 1977).

Tapahonso, Luci. *Saanii Dahataal, The Women are Singing* (Tucson: University of Arizona Press, 1993); *A Breeze Swept Through* (Albuquerque: West End Press, 1987); *Seasonal Woman* (Santa Fe: Tooth of Time Books, 1982).

Von Herzen, Lane. *Copper Crown* (New York: W. Morrow, 1991).

Weigle, Marta and Kyle Fiore. *Santa Fe and Taos: The Writers' Era, 1916-1941* (Santa Fe: Ancient City Press, 1982).

Wilbur-Cruce, Eva Antonia. *A Beautiful, Cruel Country* (Tucson: University of Arizona Press, 1987).

Wilder, Kathryn, editor. *Walking the Twilight II: Women Writers of the Southwest* (Flagstaff: Northland, 1996); *Walking the Twilight: Women Writers of the Southwest* (Flagstaff: Northland, 1994).

Williams, Terry Tempest. *Refuge: An Unnatural History of Family and Place* (New York: Pantheon, 1991); *Pieces of White Shell* (New York: Scribner, 1984).